THE LAW SCHOOL ADMISSION GAME

THE LAW SCHOOL ADMISSION GAME

PLAY LIKE AN EXPERT, THIRD EDITION

Ann K. Levine

ISBN-13: 9780983845386
ISBN-10: 0983845387
Library of Congress Control Number: 2017906915
Abraham Publishing, Santa Barbara, CA

To everyone fighting the good fight and for tomorrow's fighters.
Hoping this book helps launch you there.

CONTENTS

INTRODUCTION

So, you're applying to law school. You could choose to wing it, to do it blindly, on a leap of faith that you're smart enough to figure this out on your own. Or you could recognize that the decision to go to law school, and where to go to law school, is one that will follow you throughout your life and that putting effort into applying to law school is vital to a successful outcome. Since you're reading this book, you're well on your way to following this second—more mindful—path.

After all, the bitter lawyers (and yes, there are quite a few) are usually those who didn't do their research, didn't give themselves options, and didn't make smart decisions. Making good choices for yourself throughout the law school application process is the way to set yourself up for a happy and successful life. There is a direct correlation between applying to law school thoughtfully and the options available to you for your legal education. There is no way to wing this and get great results.

This book will help you make great decisions about every part of the law school application process. How do I know this? In part, because I've written this book before! The first edition of *The Law School Admission Game: Play Like an Expert* was published in June 2009 and spent three years as an Amazon.com bestseller. Thousands of copies sold in print, electronic, and audiobook forms. The second edition was published in 2013 in print, e-book, and audiobook form and instantly replaced its predecessor at the top of the charts. The feedback I've gotten from law school applicants through the years has been gracious, appreciative, and enthusiastic. I've even made some lifelong friends who first met me by reading a previous edition of this book. And, of course, the book is based on my experiences with law school admissions, having worked for three law schools (two as director of admissions).

And this version, the third edition—with new and updated information—is even better. Each year that I'm in this law school admissions business, I learn new things and get new ideas, which are included for your benefit. I work with an increasingly diverse group of applicants and can share their stories with you. I can include recent trends (the increasing reliance on interviews, for example) and new resources that have emerged. Since I've been working in law school admissions since 1999, you're going to obtain a lot of valuable information in a short, concise book that shouldn't take you more than four hours to read. I hope it will become a resource for you throughout your admission cycle. I recommend reading the book cover to cover at first and then creating your own checklist and timeline based on the suggestions in this book that apply to you. I also suggest referencing the relevant chapters of the book in your personal calendar (e.g., chapter 8 when it's time to work on your résumé) so that you remind yourself to reread it when it's time to tackle that aspect of your application.

In addition to providing you with insider knowledge and concrete advice about putting together your law school applications (whether you are bound for Harvard Law School, Seattle University School of Law, or anywhere in between), I have added more samples of written materials, more examples of how people have presented themselves successfully in the past, more case studies, and more quotes from people who have successfully navigated this process in the past, and I have updated the book to reflect the current climate (and mechanics of applying online through LSAC.org) for law school admissions, including an in-depth "How To" guide and a sample LSAT study schedule.

My Background

I was previously the director of admissions for two law schools approved by the American Bar Association (ABA) and have spent the last fifteen years working in the world of law school admissions. I started Law School Expert, a law school admission consulting company, in 2004. Since then,

I have helped thousands of law school applicants achieve their law school admission goals. The advice in this book benefited from the thoughts, experiences, and feedback of my many clients who have become successful law students and lawyers. The diversity of my clients, their experiences, and their results have exposed me to pretty much every possible story, background, and potential "red flag" in an application and how it can be presented most effectively in the application process. Their law school experiences have run the gamut: my clients (as a whole) have been admitted to every single ABA-approved law school.

In this book, I will answer your questions about the process of applying to law school, including the following:

1. What are law schools looking for?
2. Should I get more work experience before applying to law school?
3. What is the LSAT and how should I prepare for it?
4. How can I use my time in college to improve my chances of being admitted to law school?
5. How can I leverage my professional experience within my law school application?
6. Do I need perfect grades and a 170 LSAT score to get into law school?
7. When should I submit applications?
8. Should I apply under a binding Early Decision Program?
9. Who should write my letters of recommendation, and what makes an impactful letter of recommendation?
10. What should I write my personal statement about?
11. How do I explain a weakness in my application?
12. Can I be admitted to law school if I have to report a blemish in my background under the Character and Fitness section of an application?
13. If I attended college outside of the United States, how will law schools view my credentials?
14. Do I have to write the optional essays?
15. How do I know if I should write a diversity statement?
16. Where should I apply to law school?

17. When should I be working on my applications?
18. How do I handle a law school interview?
19. How can I improve my chances of being admitted from a waiting list?
20. Can I negotiate a scholarship offer?
21. How do I choose which law school to attend?

That's a lot of ground to cover, and even this is just the tip of the iceberg, so let's get started.

CHAPTER 1

THINKING ABOUT LAW SCHOOL

There was a time when law school was a great default option for bright college graduates who were not on the pre-med track. If you have someone paying the bill for you to attend, this may still be the case. However, in the post-2008 economy, choosing to attend law school comes with more uncertainty and necessitates a thorough review of your strengths and weaknesses, your career aspirations, your financial situation, and your prospects, given where you would be eligible to attend law school. If you have not yet done any serious research about the legal profession, what lawyers do, how much lawyers make, and how hard they work, you may want to start by reading my book, *The Law School Decision Game: A Playbook for Prospective Lawyers.*

If you are still in the investigation stage and just learning about law school and careers in law, here are some ideas to help further your exploration:

1. Take some law-related and/or writing and research–intensive courses and see how you do.
2. Attend seminars—on a college campus, at a nearby law school, or arranged through a local ABA group—to learn about areas of the law and to meet lawyers.
3. Consider shadowing a lawyer or interning with a lawyer for a better view of the daily realities of the legal profession.
4. Reach out to lawyers for informational interviews and informal meetings.

5. Take a career-assessment test.
6. If you are a nontraditional applicant (meaning you have been out of college for a significant period of time or you were an older college student), talk with friends who are lawyers and people who practice law in a way that is related to your current industry.
7. Observe court proceedings.
8. Volunteer at a legal services organization.

Skills that are relevant and helpful in the practice of law are:

1. oral and written communication skills;
2. complex reading comprehension;
3. problem-solving skills;
4. research skills;
5. people skills;
6. foreign-language proficiency;
7. business acumen;
8. willingness to work hard;
9. professional ethics; and
10. being detail oriented.

The skills most utilized by lawyers can vary according to the type of practice. While litigators need to be writers and orators, they may also need knowledge of medical records or accounting documents. Transactional attorneys not only need to be wordsmiths, but may also need people skills to be deal-makers. (For more about different areas of law, see *The Law School Decision Game*).

Once you've completed your explorations and decided to apply to law school, it's essential to understand the different elements of the application process and the time and planning they require. If you try to go directly from the "deciding" phase to the "applying" phase, you're likely to make poor decisions along the way, diminishing the options available to you. It's also important to understand what law schools value in a candidate, so that you can plan accordingly. Certain factors are seen as reliable predictors of success in law school—particularly your undergraduate GPA and your LSAT score. As of this printing, Harvard Law School announced a pilot program where applicants can choose to provide a GRE score instead of an LSAT score, and there are murmurs of Chicago-area law schools considering whether to follow suit. Even so, you'll have to take *some* standardized test that the law schools will use to judge how you might perform as a law student at their institution. These "numbers" are often the best indicator of whether you can expect to pass the bar exam (the test given by each state in order to practice law).

Your numbers are important to law schools because, in addition to helping them judge whether you'll be successful in law school, they have to feed their data regarding admitted students to the ABA, and this is the data U.S. News & World Report uses to determine law school rankings. Law schools watch these rankings closely, since applicants and hiring entities also watch them closely. However, this is not to say that law schools never make exceptions to the numbers; it just means that the numbers often guide them, and your credentials and experiences will be considered in conjunction with the hard data when law schools make admissions decisions.

As you go through the application process, it's important to cultivate resources you can trust, eliminating "fake news" in order to make sound decisions. See where the advice is coming from before you take it. It's also important to remember that not all advice applies universally. Guidance given to someone who will most likely go to Harvard or Stanford would not necessarily apply to someone who hopes to go part-time at a local law school while supporting a family. In addition, legal education (including the cost of obtaining your Juris Doctor (JD) degree) has changed a lot in the last ten to fifteen years, so the advice you are given may be outdated. If you are still a year or more out from applying to law school and you are currently enrolled in college, here are some suggestions:

1. Since your GPA is still within your control, work hard. Pick classes that interest and excite you, and do well in the most challenging classes you can. It helps to have a sincere interest in the subject matter. People tend to perform better if they are engaged in what they are learning. It's not necessary to major in history or political science. But if your classes are on a topic like music or the

sciences, or even on classics, taking a class or two in a law-related topic will help you (1) show interest in the subject matter and (2) decide whether law school is really something that interests you. And, if your grades are borderline for the school of your choice, performing well in a law-related course will show your potential in similar courses in law school. Taking a law-centered class will also make your choices look less random when you submit a law school application.

Many law schools will forgive a poor start if you redeem yourself during your last two years of college. If you really need to show an upward trend, consider taking a gap year after college so that law schools will be able to consider grades from your senior year. This should also give you time to cultivate faculty letters of recommendation.

2. Build relationships with your professors to get excellent and, substantive, recommendations. Take the initiative to visit them during office hours, to take more than one class with a professor, and/or to assist with a professor's research. And speak up during class. Not only will you get stronger letters of recommendation, but you will also benefit more fully from your educational experience. This can be difficult at large public universities—or if you are a transfer student or spent significant time studying abroad—so planning ahead of time pays off.

"One great way to get noticed is to speak to the professor at the very beginning of the course. When I returned to undergrad after being in the navy, I only had a few semesters (and limited courses) left before graduation, so I didn't have much time to build a relationship with a professor. Instead, I approached my professors at the beginning of my courses and explained my goal of attending law school and that I hoped to earn a letter of recommendation from them by demonstrating my work in their class. This worked well for me. They watched me more closely and certainly remembered me come the end of the semester when I asked for a recommendation. Each professor seemed impressed by my assertiveness and was more than happy to provide a strong letter on my behalf. Of course, this only works if you're really prepared to kick butt in their class," says Lauren Morina, a current law student at Washington and Lee.

3. Law schools value engagement in your community but avoid joining anything just because you think it looks good on your law school application. Members of Phi Alpha Delta are a dime a dozen. If something really interests you, become an active leader in a related organization. Whether it's a cultural or political organization, student government, a volunteer group, or athletics, think about how you demonstrate leadership, growth, teamwork, and dedication, rather than simply collecting memberships in a number of groups. Go for depth over breadth. Explore opportunities outside of your comfort zone. Your sorority or fraternity should not be the only thing on your résumé.

4. Find your niche. Consider your reasons before signing up; don't just do what you feel you're supposed to do. Be honest with yourself. Choosing activities isn't about giving your mom bragging rights at dinners with her friends. It's about deciding what you like, what you're good at, what you'd like to know more about, and how you can grow from different activities. When you observe your experiences candidly, what do you see? What portrait have you painted? And, importantly, where are you missing out on formative, crucial experiences? Are you someone who never really had to earn your own pocket money? You might benefit from real roll-up-your-sleeves work experience at the campus Starbucks. Do you appear to lack intellectual curiosity or gravitas? Maybe there's a research opportunity or a thesis topic to explore or a way to tutor other students. If you've always had the "right" internships with your member of Congress, consider getting involved at the grassroots level, providing services to others. One law school decision maker told me, "We are looking for work ethic and a sincere interest in the study of law. We want to see how the experiences a person has had led them to the conclusion that law school was the next logical step...not necessarily how many internships they have had in (judicial) chambers or work through a law firm." Use the opportunities presented to you in college to explore things that really interest

you, no matter how prestigious they may seem to others. Test your boundaries and stretch your horizons. Interact with people whose backgrounds are different from your own, and figure out what you care about and what motivates you. Taking time for introspection now will not only benefit your law school applications but also encourage personal growth. This will, in turn, help you make good decisions about your future, even if they end up leading you away from law school.

5. Conduct yourself professionally and responsibly. This includes how you present yourself on social networking sites. Enforce your privacy settings. Many of my clients change their names on Facebook while they are applying to law school and, while this confuses me greatly when I scroll through my newsfeed, I think it's a smart idea. Law schools are increasingly reviewing online sources, and it's better to be smart, especially if you're applying for prestigious scholarships or if you have character and fitness issues that would cause law schools to have concerns about you from your application materials. One law school admission decision maker shared with me the following story: "I will never forget reading a beautifully written essay about the experience of a student in a rural community...the hardships, the lack of resources...how it tested them...and then went online for my social media check and found picture after picture of them partying in said rural area and disparaging remarks made by their friends about the rural communities...Guilt by association and lack of judgment on social media—not impressive." Harvard College recently made headlines by rescinding admission offers to ten undergraduates who posted inappropriate content online. Law schools, likewise, are looking for people who exercise good judgment. Use of social media is a great place for them to test for that.

6. Stay out of trouble. Be careful about your conduct in the dorms and around campus. There's no reason to fight with your dormitory's resident assistant and get a discipline record over a noise violation. Show that you exercise good judgment by not finding yourself in situations where you are getting citations for

underage drinking, use of fake IDs, public urination, and other indiscretions—like a domestic violence call for arguing with your boyfriend outside a bar. If this advice is coming too late, make up for it by taking responsibility for your actions and not becoming a repeat offender (see Chapter 7, Explaining Your Weaknesses, for more on this topic).

7. Spend your summers wisely. Explore different careers. Explore the world. Not everything on your résumé needs to have a direct connection with law: business skills are important, global awareness is important, compassion and service are important. Learning how to function in a professional environment, live on your own far from home, relate to others who are different from you, speak a foreign language, and even save money for a certain goal (like next semester's tuition or your study abroad semester) are worthy activities. If you decide to work in a law firm, take the initiative to do more than just file and answer phones. Take the time to actually talk with attorneys about what they do—and observe them in their non-glamorous moments. Turn everything into a learning experience, and you will grow and expand your horizons, adding value to your future endeavors. After all, doing interesting things gives you something to discuss during your next job interview. So, whatever you do, don't phone it in—engage with it!

8. Consider taking time off before law school. I am often asked, "Will law schools like me better if I take a year or two off before applying?" If your grades need to show another year of improvement and/or you need more time to prepare for the LSAT, it can, absolutely, benefit your admission chances to wait a year. However, grades and LSAT being equal, there is no clear preference for an applicant who takes time off and one who goes to law school straight from college. Even Northwestern Law, which spends a lot of time discussing the value of work experience in applicants, takes people straight out of college. On the other hand, *Yale Daily News* reported in 2011 that only 20 percent of the entering first-year class at Yale Law School came straight from college (yaledailynews.com/blog/2011/

gap-years-strengthen-law-school-plans/). Harvard Law School recently announced a deferral program for people who apply as juniors in college and who pledge, if admitted to Harvard Law, to take two years off to work or pursue a fellowship before attending the law school.

Some of the benefits to taking time off include:

1. showing an upward trend in grades;
2. saving money for law school;
3. deciding what you want to do with your life/career; and
4. taking classes and/or having jobs that will garner positive letters of recommendation.

Here are some words of wisdom from people who attended law school after spending time in the professional world:

- "My work experience definitely helped me outperform my GPA at OCI [on-campus interviews for summer law jobs]—I had multiple offers from V25 firms where I was below their GPA median. The person interviewing you at OCI looks at twenty identical résumés a day—having work experience is almost a relief for them—they get to talk about something other than what you did in college" (3L at Georgetown Law).
- "Going from undergrad to having to face time with high-level BigLaw lawyers is intimidating. It's definitely a struggle trying to figure out how to be taken seriously and not looked at as a 'kid' if all you know is school. I always noticed my classmates who worked, even for two to three years before coming to law school, seemed to shine when talking to professors and attorneys at job fairs/OCI." (Dan Ferrett, who now works at the Financial Industry Regulatory Authority after graduating from the Catholic University School of Law).
- "It was the best thing I ever did: more maturity, ability to treat law school like a job (going in from nine to six), better understanding of what type of law you want to practice, and a ton more talking points in interviews" (2L at Georgetown Law).

- Having professional experience can also help you manage your time during law school, according to Nathan Fox of Fox Test Prep. "Law school can easily overrun your life, if you let it. I'd frequently see the twenty-one-year-olds having frantic, unproductive study groups at 11:00 p.m. However, one of my friends drew a box around law school and dominated. He was a bit older, with real-world experience, and he simply turned law school into a forty-hour, Monday–Friday workweek. He never took his books home once during the entire 1L year. He'd show up at 9:00 a.m. every day, even if he only had one class in the afternoon. When he wasn't in class, he was in the library reading. He left at 5:00 p.m., slamming his books in his locker. Unsurprisingly, he got awesome grades. It was a classy way to do it."

- One of my clients was admitted to Stanford Law School and was all set to go. Instead, she deferred admission for two years and took a job as a paralegal in a civil rights firm. She sees immense value in this experience. "I learned how the law is actually practiced, how litigators live their lives, and both the excitement and challenges that come from being a practicing lawyer. This experience guided my decisions in law school (which clinics to pursue, what clerkships to accept) and gave me a much clearer sense of what I wanted to do with my law degree," she said.

- Another client told me that "you can't know if yet more school (and debt) is the right choice unless you experience life outside of school."

- "I scored my in-house position (after a four-year stint in BigLaw) in part due to working as a paralegal in-house before law school" (Larissa Leibowitz, who graduated from Northwestern Law).

- "Taking time off was one of the best decisions I've ever made; I'm so glad I did it. By my senior year, I was feeling burned out and the prospect of going straight to three years of law school felt daunting. I was also scared that if I went directly to law school, then I would be putting myself on this track (of going to law school and working super hard and then having some crazy job during both summers and then getting a job and working crazy hours) that I wouldn't be able to get off of, and so, mentally, it was really good for me to pause things and have a year to take a breath. I also used this year to volunteer and travel and get the experience of being a young professional in a city where I had previously only been a full-time student. I also used the time I've had to really think about what I might want to do with my law degree and how I can set myself up to do that" (2L student).

- "I am finding that my prior work experience has been the sole reason why I am getting any interest from employers. I had an interview last week where the interviewer said, 'Normally we only look at people from more prestigious schools, but you clearly can do the work because you've done it before.' Granted, I am only looking at jobs where my prior experience would be relevant (i.e., energy law)" (Benjamin Piiru, a 1L student at Loyola Chicago School of Law).

- "It was 100 percent helpful to have had two years of work experience before law school, especially when trying to apply for clerkships. Because judges are hiring so early these days, applicants will not have had summer internships yet. Therefore, the only benchmark many judges will have for whether someone will be a good employee (rather than just thinker) is whether they developed maturity through prior work experience" (3L at Stanford Law).

Already Out of College? Planning for Your Law School Application Process as a Non-Traditional Applicant

1. Think about how you're going to manage the time it will take you to prepare for the LSAT and apply to law school and how you will manage your work and personal responsibilities. It's important not to underestimate the effort. If you are working full-time or caring for children, you may only have five to ten hours each week to prepare for the LSAT, so you will need more than three months to prepare. And, if it's been a long time since you've taken a standardized test and/or if you typically struggle

with standardized exams, you'll want to give yourself perhaps six months or more to get yourself ready. Often, older applicants feel a great hurry to start law school as soon as possible, but the opportunities you will have regarding what law school you can get into and whether you will be competitive for scholarships will depend on your LSAT score, especially if your college performance is unimpressive.

2. Look for people who would be able to write letters of recommendation. You may want to begin reaching out to former professors from college or graduate school and/or former employers. If you are working but not comfortable letting your employer know that you are thinking of leaving, then you will need to think creatively about people who will be qualified to write about your academic and/or professional abilities. You may need to add a volunteer position or a class to your responsibilities. This would be helpful for a stay-at-home parent who is applying to law school as well (see chapter 8 for more on letters of recommendation).

3. Save money. LSAT preparation and applications (and admission consulting!) add up quickly, and that's before you think about saving money for law school itself. Traveling to visit schools, and perhaps even buying your first suit, should be part of your budget as well.

4. Attend online webinars and chats with the law schools you are considering to get a better sense of what they have to offer and to ask questions about programs and opportunities suited to your interests.

5. Research your prospective career, and modify your expectations accordingly. Older applicants face a different set of issues when deciding whether a law career is feasible given their family demands, financial situation, and the age at which they hope to retire. The expense of attending law school is an even bigger deterrent for those who have fewer working years ahead of them. Indeed, some career options—like being a first-year associate at a large law firm, where billing expectations are high and it takes longer to assume meaningful responsibility for cases—may be less attractive to older people.

CHAPTER 2

GETTING READY TO APPLY

Here is What You Need to Do to Apply to Law School

1. You must have a bachelor's degree before you matriculate in law school.

2. Register for Credential Assembly Service (CAS) through the Law School Admission Council (LSAC), and send your transcripts here. You may need to send more transcripts than you think. (See the LSAC "How To" Guide for concrete instructions on registering with LSAC and completing the necessary steps in the Appendix). If you have transcripts from a foreign institution you'll have to send them through a separate evaluation service through LSAC.

3. Cultivate recommender relationships, and ask for letters of recommendation (see Chapter 5).

4. Check your Academic Summary Report (based on your transcripts) for errors/inconsistencies.

5. Take the LSAT, which is currently offered four times per year, but is slated to be offered six times in 2018-2019 and may be offered more often in digital form afterward. (Changes with the LSAT are happening so quickly that I had to re-write certain sections of this book after it had already been edited for publication, so keep on top of changes by subscribing to my newsletter through LawSchoolExpert.com). You need to choose an LSAT

date and reserve a seat in advance. Select an LSAT Prep method that works for your learning style and budget. You must take the LSAT and have a score within three years (this is true for most schools, though a few will accept a score received within the past five years [see Chapter 4]). (At the time of this printing, two law schools are accepting applications with a GRE score for those who don't have an LSAT score. More law schools may follow suit in the coming months and years. However, I will assume that readers are applying to more than just Arizona and Harvard Law and will, in fact, need to take the LSAT).

6. Collect fee waivers, and explore schools by registering for the Credential Referral Service through LSAC and attending a law school forum or law school fair on a campus near you.

7. Create your résumé (see Chapter 8).

8. Write your personal statement (see Chapter 9).

9. Draft other application materials, including addenda (see Chapter 7) and optional essays (see Chapter 10).

10. Create a list of schools, essay prompts, and requirements as per the application instructions and each school's website (see Chapter 11, Deciding Where to Apply).

11. Fill out and submit applications.

12. Complete any interviews that are either open to all applicants or that you are invited to do (see Chapter 12, Preparing for Interviews).

13. Complete FAFSA for need-based financial aid, usually in January of the year you plan to start law school.

Rolling Admissions and the Application Timeline

Timing matters: you have a better chance of getting into law school earlier in the cycle. Law school applications become available between the end of August and the beginning of October, with most schools accepting applications after Labor Day. Deadlines are somewhere between February 1 and June 1 for each school. However, law schools start admitting people shortly after applications become available (in October and

November), so if you wait to apply right before deadlines, schools may have already admitted enough people to fill their classes and begun creating waiting lists. As a result, unless your application is stellar, and with high numbers for that school, it's hard to be competitive for admission late in the application cycle. When people talk about "rolling admissions," this is what they mean—your chances of admission improve the earlier you apply.

When Should You Submit Your Applications?

If you take the June LSAT, apply in September for admission the following year. If you take the September LSAT, apply in November. If you take the November LSAT (2018 and later), apply by early January. If you take the December LSAT, apply in January. Taking the LSAT at the end of January (2018 and later) or in February to start law school the same year puts you at a disadvantage. Check for February 1 deadlines at some schools. Be aware that not all schools will accept the January or February LSAT for admission that fall. Taking the March LSAT (2018 and later) should be for the following admission cycle and not for beginning law school that fall.

Taking the June LSAT to start law school the same fall is a horrible plan. You won't have your LSAT score until July and school starts in August. Even if a school claims to accept June LSAT scores, by August they probably know whether they will be taking any stragglers from the waiting list, and they will get priority over your application.

The LSAT dates for 2018-2019 are scheduled for June 11, September 8, November 17, January 26, March 30 and June 3. The earlier date in September and moving the December LSAT to November will help applicants with rolling admissions, as will moving the February LSAT to the end of January. The March 30 and June 3 dates should *not* be used for people hoping to start law school in the fall of the same year. These dates may change for later admission cycles, and the LSAT may be offered more regularly after June 2019 if the digital version of the test is up and running. Even if that is the case, the timing described above will still be useful in helping you to pick an ideal time to take the LSAT.

Is There an Advantage to Applying on the Very First Day?

No. Applying on the first day applications are released versus a month (or even two) later does not cause any difference in your admission result.

Law school admission officers spend most of August through November at recruiting events (giving out precious fee waivers and trying to drum up interest in their schools). It's hard to spend much time in September reviewing files. Back when I was a young director of admission, I was on the bus with all of the other admission officers, bouncing from Marriott to Marriott, lugging heavy brochures and standing behind tables, answering questions from potential applicants for hours at a time. I was not reading files during my free time.

Besides, it's a better idea to take a few extra weeks to submit the highest quality product and the best possible personal statement and résumé, rather than rush. Any applications submitted before Thanksgiving are considered early in the cycle.

If you are sticking with a June LSAT score, submit your applications in September-October. If you are working with a September LSAT score, submit applications in October-November (you can absolutely make Early Decision and Early Notification deadlines with a September LSAT score if you plan ahead). If you're taking the LSAT in November or December, plan to submit applications by mid-January. Taking the LSAT later than this will make it harder for you to get into schools, even where your numbers are in range with the medians for that school. You are more likely to be declined or wait-listed, and there will be fewer scholarship dollars available at that time of year. However, if you really rock the LSAT, then midrange schools will often find a place for you. Be realistic, however: reach schools will be even more of a reach at that time of year.

Should You Apply before Having Your LSAT Score?

Usually, no. Your application will not be reviewed until it is "complete," and it can't be complete without an LSAT score. Therefore, there is no advantage in submitting your application without it. So, unless you're up against a deadline (as can happen with the February LSAT, but will be less likely to happen once the LSAT moves to January), wait until you have your score to submit your application.

Besides, until the score comes in, you don't know if you'll even be competitive at any given school. You might save money by not applying to a school that you know you don't need to apply to anymore (safety school) or by not applying to a school that turns out to be a far greater reach for your numbers than you might have predicted.

In addition, if you submit the application before knowing your score, you may miss the opportunity to explain your LSAT score as part of your application. For example, you can't submit an explanation that says, "My first score was low but my second score, after reducing my work schedule, was higher" if you don't actually know that it *was* higher.

Remember that it currently takes three to four weeks after you take the LSAT to get your score. Once you have your score, you may decide to apply to different schools and/or to retake the LSAT and postpone your applications. Keep in mind that this often makes the most sense. If you get your September score, and it's five points lower than your consistent practice exam scores, then it's worth waiting and taking the December test (applying in January) for a five-point improvement in your score. This could change the schools you get into and the amount of scholarships you might receive, so it would be worth the downside of applying slightly later in the admission cycle.

What Is the Latest Date You Can Apply and Still Take Advantage of Rolling Admissions?

When I wrote the first version of this book in 2009, law school application numbers were at an all-time high, and I stressed the importance of applying by December in order to be competitive. For the 2013 cycle, however, I had more clients still applying in January and February, and that was perfectly acceptable considering that (at that time) applications to law school had decreased 38 percent over the previous two years. In the 2017 cycle, schools waited for December LSAT takers to make the majority of their decisions.

Remember that anyone taking the November or December LSAT is probably spending the winter holidays on application materials. It can be stressful to find time to work on applications with family demands and, of course, it's usually storm and flu season, which can hamper things. Plan ahead, and don't save everything for winter break. There are schools that ask you to apply before a date in January to be considered for certain scholarships, so keep your eye on those deadlines too. See, for example, www.law.nyu.edu/admissions/jdadmissions/applicants/applications/index.htm

The January/February LSAT, however, is still putting you very late in the admission cycle, delaying your results and making it both *less* likely that you'll get into reach schools and *more* likely that you'll be wait-listed at schools you may have gotten into by applying earlier in the cycle. My February LSAT takers who apply in March generally get into some safety schools and are wait-listed at some of those schools as well. However, they do not get into reach schools. Additionally, the scholarship offers are definitely not what they would have been had the application been timely.

If you decide to take the January/February LSAT the same year that you hope to start law school, take some time to consider an alternative strategy. If you are graduating from college, it might be good to take a year off and let schools see your senior year grades and to gain some work/travel/volunteer experience while giving yourself more time to put applications together and study for the LSAT. Older applicants often worry about getting another year older and delaying law school; they often feel rushed to apply and go wherever they are admitted. But this is often a poor decision in the long term, especially where insufficient time has been spent preparing for the LSAT and perfecting application materials. Besides, taking a year to save some money for law school would be a sound, long-term decision. If you've been recently laid off and you need to be in school for the loans, please reconsider your decision. Law school is a huge investment, and **you** need to be invested in the process, taking the time to make sure that this is really a sound financial/career direction for you.

Every year, people comment on my blog and Facebook page telling me they are taking the June LSAT to start law school in the fall, saying they haven't had time to prepare but it's absolutely crucial – "everything is riding on this" – that they start law school immediately. I can't imagine a situation where this would be true, and I've heard it all! Law school is never the answer to a life crisis. Just this week, someone posted in an LSAT page on Facebook that she needed last minute studying tips for the LSAT – 48 hours before the test – and when I responded that she didn't sound ready for the test and that she should wait until September, she went after me for not knowing the full situation and for judging her. (Of course, she probably didn't expect that I'd written books on this topic). The point is that I don't need to know her circumstances because I can detect whether someone is going to law school with eyes wide open. When people approach the LSAT in this way, I know that these are the individuals who choose to attend less reputable law schools because it's where they could get in, and these are the people who will be taking out the full amount in loans, who will be academically dismissed from law school, and/or who will fail to pass the bar exam upon graduation.

For more on whether law school is the right decision for you, take time to read *The Law School Decision Game*. I am a big believer in making the smarter, long-term decision over the convenient, short-term one. After all, it's usually the people who applied at the last minute and chose to attend whatever law school would take them who try to transfer the following year. But unless you have grades at the top of your 1L class, it's very hard to transfer.

What Is An "Early Decision Program"?

One of the first decisions you'll have to make after finalizing your schools list is whether to apply under an Early Decision Program. These programs usually have early deadlines and require you to state that you will absolutely and unequivocally attend if you are granted admission by a certain date. If you are accepted, you withdraw all other applications and send your deposit.

The rule with Early Decision applications is that this is a **binding agreement** you are making with the school; if admitted, you **will attend** that school and withdraw all applications from other schools. In return, you will receive your admission decision a little bit faster and often have a better shot at getting into a reach school. But you have to be sure you're willing to walk away from a scholarship offer to another school to do this. While some Early Decision programs come with scholarship offers, these programs are usually intended to "steal" applicants from higher-ranked schools and are actually more competitive than applying under regular decision.

Keep in mind you can only apply **binding to one school at a time**. Consider school deadlines for Early Decision: Columbia's may be November 15, but you would find out in time to apply binding to schools with two rounds of Early Decision or later Early Decision deadlines, including (as of this printing) University of Virginia, University of Pennsylvania, Cornell University, or Georgetown University Law Center—("GULC"), all schools with later Early Decision applications. (In fact, Georgetown's extends until March).

Most law school applicants do *not* apply binding anywhere. I advise most of my clients to keep their options open. But, I've had a number of low-LSAT/high-GPA clients admitted to GULC because they applied binding. So if your goal is to get into the best-ranked law school, no matter what it will cost you, then this can work well for you. This may change in future admission cycles, given that Georgetown's ranking recently slid just outside of the top fourteen for the first time in recent memory, so they may start watching their LSATs more closely in the next few admission cycles to counteract this.

There is an advantage for law schools to grab some strong applicants without worrying about "yield"—the ratio of students who are admitted (acceptance rate) versus those who actually attend. Instead of admitting a lot of students with low numbers and having some not attend, they can take these applicants under a binding program and protect their perceived selectivity. If a school can handle a certain number of people with LSATs in the 153–160 range, then accepting them through Early Decision benefits the school. It also helps them fill some seats without having to recruit heavily. It's such a benefit to schools that a few are sweetening the deal further. Binding applicants to George Washington, for example, can choose the competitive scholarship track (making it harder to get in but guaranteeing money) or the regular Early Decision Program. Northwestern also has a binding program that comes with a scholarship, rendering an early admission even more challenging (see http://www.law.northwestern.edu/admissions/applying/earlydecision.html).

What Do Law Schools Do with My Application?

The first thing a law school does when receiving your application is check to make sure it is complete. Are the questions answered properly? Did you attach the correct documents? Did you leave any questions blank? Then the school waits for your LSAC Credential Assembly Service Report, which includes your LSAT score(s), transcripts, Academic Summary Report (presenting information from your transcripts as a cover sheet to your actual transcripts, including your GPA), and the letters of recommendation you have designated for that school. CAS forwards these items as they receive them, so even if you haven't taken the LSAT yet, they will go ahead and send the other items. However, the law school won't do a single thing with your file until it has everything it needs.

Once your application is deemed "complete," it will most likely be put into one of three piles. At many schools, these piles are based on index numbers. The index calculation is based on your LSAT (the highest at most schools but the average at a few schools) and undergraduate GPA. Based simply on the numbers, your file will be a "presumptive admit," "presumptive deny," or somewhere in the middle, designated as—a "committee file" (Obviously, the applications are online, and schools aren't really printing them out and putting them into files and aren't creating piles of paper files any more, but this is the easiest way to explain how they are coded and distinguished from one another at first glance).

At most schools, the director of admissions makes most decisions single handedly. One dean of admissions told me that it's common for only 10 percent of files to be forwarded to the faculty committee. This was certainly my experience as director of admissions for two law schools. If your numbers make you a presumptive admit, then someone in the admission office will review your file. If everything is strong, and there are no red flags, signs of weirdness or arrogance, or character and fitness violations, you'll probably be admitted right off the bat. Easy! If there are some concerns, your file will be passed along to the committee (see below).

If your numbers place you in the presumptive deny pile, then someone in the admission office will read through your application for soft factors, explanations, review of your essay(s), résumé, letters of recommendation, etc. If something catches the reader's eye, you will be bumped up for committee review. This happens frequently. However, if your numbers are low, and there are problems with your application and/or candidacy beyond the numbers, you will no longer be in the running. Watch out for the online status checker to say, "decision mailed" (I'm kidding; decision mailed doesn't *always* mean you struck out. Usually acceptances are e-mailed or you may even receive a phone call).

If you are in the committee pile, then someone in the admissions office takes some notes and passes the file along to members of the faculty admission committee for their review, comments, and votes. This takes a while because faculty members on the whole are not a speedy bunch. They have classes and vacations and those pesky office hours and faculty meetings. But this is where your file gets ranked as someone who will be admitted, wait-listed, held for a later decision, or rejected.
This process explains why two people whose applications are complete on the same day may receive decisions months apart from each other.

Once you are admitted, your file is reviewed for scholarship consideration. Sometimes you are notified of a scholarship offer at the time of acceptance, and sometimes this comes later.

How Do I Get a Scholarship to Law School?

Most scholarships are given based on merit alone; there is no separate application. A few schools use separate scholarship applications for public-interest scholarships or very focused (and very prestigious) opportunities, but most schools will let you know about scholarship offers at the same time (or shortly after) they offer you admission. You can guess which schools will offer you scholarships based on how competitive your numbers are; indeed, schools use scholarships to motivate people with higher numbers to attend. Lower-ranked schools also liberally use scholarships to encourage people to attend, period. Some schools, including Harvard and Stanford, only offer need-based aid.

Scholarships range in amount from, approximately, $5,000–$40,000 per year. However, these generous offers often have important conditions attached to them. It's essential to look at the renewability criteria for any scholarship and ask about the likelihood of it being renewed. Is the required GPA for keeping the scholarship a 2.3 or is it a 3.3? A 3.3 might sound like a low threshold by undergraduate standards, but in law school, that places you in the top third of your class. And you can't assume that just because you are a "merit scholarship" recipient, you would *of course* be in the top third of your law school class. You should ask a law school what percentage of scholarship recipients end up keeping them after the first year of law school. Moreover, you should also be wary of "scholarship stacking," in which students on scholarships are placed in classes together—furthering the competition to keep one's funding.

Even if you are pulled off a waiting list, you still might receive a scholarship because (1) more funds are available because of people who turned down their spots in the class and (2) law schools want to seal the deal and solidify their classes.

You can negotiate scholarships, but you need to be gentle about it, and you need to have a plan. Schools are sensitive to being used: they know you might be asking for more money from them simply to get another school to math their offer. When negotiating scholarships, here are some important things to keep in mind:

- You want to demonstrate your strong interest in the school. It's even better if you can say that an increased scholarship offer would guarantee your acceptance of their offer, and you would immediately send in a deposit and/or withdraw all other applications, etc. "I got Penn up from a 'final offer' by saying that I'd consider it, but if they could offer me $X more, then I'd commit immediately," said Rebecca Sivitz.
- It's good to have a specific number in mind. Will $2,500 more really make a difference for you? Or would you need a certain amount because a similarly ranked law school in your hometown would allow you to live at home and save money?
- Present the school with one or two select scholarship offers from schools that are similarly ranked and similarly situated or, even better, ranked higher.
- Be polite about it. Don't sound arrogant, demanding, or entitled. I had a client who sent a pretty obnoxious e-mail to UCLA (without running it past me first!) about the great offers Duke and USC gave him, and the Dean at UCLA essentially replied, "Well, then, good luck at Duke or USC." My client panicked;

UCLA really was one of his top choices (Don't worry, I talked him through fixing the problem, but trust me: this isn't a situation you want to find yourself in).

- If the scholarship (or increase) really wouldn't make the difference in getting you to attend, then it becomes a game. If law schools smell that, they will be happy to see you go to a different school.
- Don't exaggerate your offers from other schools. Law schools will check their facts. Wake Forest will call William and Mary and ask, "Did you really give Joe Smith $30,000 a year?"

When Should You Expect to Hear Back?

Some schools are awesome about getting back to you quickly. Duke Law, and their ten-day priority application (although you have to jump through a few hoops to make it official for yield protection purposes, including a "scholarship" interview), and the University of Miami come to mind. Others will keep you waiting even past the April deadline that they give themselves for responding to applicants. If your file is "clean" (without any "red flags" or issues that require further consideration) and your numbers are solid for a school (at or above the medians), then you will probably hear back within eight to twelve weeks of applying. If you responded affirmatively—saying "yes" or checking the box that you had these items to report—on any character and fitness questions (see Chapter 7), then your application will take longer because more people will have to sign off on it before a decision is made. Of course, some schools don't review applications for a while, and they send out result letters in batches, usually because they are understaffed.

Key Takeaways

- Make yourself a timeline.
- Aim to apply early in the admission cycle.
- Consider whether a binding application is right for you.

CHAPTER 3

UNDERSTANDING YOUR GPA

T
he two most important factors in law school admissions are your undergraduate GPA and your LSAT score. Each law school keeps statistics on their students, how they perform in law school, and the extent to which their entering credentials were in line with how they ended up performing. Law schools can actually use these statistics to determine your likelihood of success in law school and the likelihood that you will pass the bar on the first try. Generally, law schools want to make solid bets: will you be able to compete in the classroom given who else will be there? You need something (LSAT or GPA usually) to make the case that you can, in fact, compete.

Your undergraduate cumulative GPA is the thing that measures your performance over the longest period of time, on skills that are most relevant to determining how you might perform in law school. Law school is academically rigorous, after all, and grades *should be* the best indicator of how you will perform in law school (although this certainly isn't true universally, and law schools appreciate that, especially if you've been out of school a long time or experienced a blip while in school that brought down your overall GPA). You must send *all of your transcripts* (with exceptions for unique circumstances as noted on LSAC's website) to LSAC for evaluation. They will be evaluated to prevent people from being at an advantage due to their school's grading system. Your grades are then calculated in a way that averages repeated course grades and includes transfer credits, creating your LSAC cumulative GPA. This will be presented in your Academic Summary Report, and your transcripts will accompany the report.

Whether you apply to law school while still in college or many years later, law schools care about your undergraduate degree. Three things matter the most:

- the school you attended;
- the subjects you studied; and
- how you performed (which is, of course, pretty important).

These are all part of the subjective consideration of the number that LSAC has calculated to be your GPA. In addition, extenuating factors as discussed in other chapters (military service, family responsibilities, illness, being a student athlete, etc.) help schools consider these three main subjective factors in context.

The School You Attended

The caliber of school you attended is important. Harvard will not view a 4.0 from the University of Phoenix the same way it will view a 4.0 (or even a 2.9, for that matter) from Dartmouth, no matter how you spin it. Remember though, that the lower you go down the rankings food chain, the less this matters. But let's start by looking at different groupings of schools, and I'll show you how a couple of my clients fared in this more recent admission cycle.

First let me tell you the stories of several clients from this recent admission cycle who all had 167 LSAT scores and how they fared at T-15 schools (keeping in mind that they didn't all apply to the same schools):

- C (3.4 Columbia): admitted to New York University, Berkeley, and Cornell, and currently wait-listed at Harvard
- Y (3.7 UCSB): admitted to UCLA, Georgetown, and USC, and currently wait-listed at NYU (applied binding)
- B (3.97 SUNY): wait-listed at Cornell, Duke, and Penn

Now, let me just insert an aside: this phenomenon *of course* perpetuates the cycle of people of privilege getting into the most elite schools. And I am not someone who believes that elite schools are the end-all-be-all. I have clients who choose full scholarships over Harvard, and I'm proud of them for making the right choice for their own lives. If you feel you'll never get ahead in life without a top law school, I highly recommend reading *Where You Go Is Not Who You Will Be* by Frank Bruni. It is written with college admissions in mind, but serves as a good reminder that many of those whom we hope to emulate came from schools we've (most likely) never heard of before. As a funny comment to this, last week my husband and I were having dinner with a high-powered couple we'd just met. We were all discussing our careers and discovered that the husband and I both went to the University of Miami. Here we were, living in Santa Barbara, California, sending our kids to the same private school and meeting to share tips about a vacation destination from which they had just returned, and there was not an Ivy League degree among us.

So, without getting too hung up on where you went to school, know that law schools are looking at the caliber of school you attended when judging your academic performance (And later, when you're deciding where to attend law school, we will keep this in mind).

The Subject(s) You Studied

Law schools want to see that, when challenged academically, you rise to the occasion. There are two aspects to this: the academic challenge and the rising to the occasion. Therefore, having an easier major and higher grades is not the perfect solution. There is no one perfect major that all law schools want to see; in fact, they want to enroll people from different academic backgrounds. But it's important to show your education helped you develop critical thinking skills, writing and research skills, and intellectual curiosity. Whether you studied music or chemistry or business, the most important thing to demonstrate is that you do well at the things you undertake. Below is a summary of different types of undergraduate majors and how law schools view them. I share this not to make you paranoid about your choices but to show you what concerns law schools may have so that you can think about perceived weaknesses, to overcome which you may need to use the personal statement and/or addendum.

Political Science, Criminal Justice, and Legal Studies

If you majored in political science, history, philosophy, or a related field, you should have two advantages: (1) a clear demonstration of your long-standing interest in law and (2) a good GPA. If you wrote a thesis, even better. This shows that you performed meaningful writing and research and approached your studies in a focused and serious way. However, if you don't have the good GPA, and you don't have a compelling reason for that (see Chapter 7, Explaining Your Weaknesses), then you will need to show seriousness of purpose and focus in another way (student leadership, internships, etc.).

A major in criminal justice is the trade school end of the pre-law major spectrum, especially since prestigious universities do not offer it as a major, and it's intended more for people who aspire to become law enforcement and probation officers. However, if you are applying for a public-interest program or scholarship, then your study of these issues could be seen as a positive factor in your applications.

Classics/Divinity/Philosophy/History

Any major that shows you're a thinker and a writer is one that law schools will respect. Doing significant research with a professor and/or a thesis helps bolster your street cred as a serious academic in fields that are similar to—and often touch upon—law. These majors involve reading a lot of dense material, thinking about it, interpreting it, and making an argument based upon it. Philosophy and history in particular give you the opportunity to choose courses and paper topics that are law-related to both explore and demonstrate your interest in law.

Philosophy is the more intellectual cousin of the pre-law majors, and if you do well with philosophy (and with actually making an argument with a conclusion, rather than simply raising more questions), then it shows an academic affinity for law school. This is especially true at the more selective universities and high LSAT levels—the top ten law schools definitely see a philosophy major as preparation for an academic career path (e.g., becoming a law professor). And, if your less-selective school is especially known for its philosophy department, such as Rutgers, law schools recognize this, and it's a way to overcome any perceived weakness in the school you attended.

Science/Math/Engineering

Your GPA may be lower (but at least a 3.0) and still be impressive because of difficult courses and extended lab hours. This background will be especially helpful if you want to go into patent or intellectual property law. If you are worried about how your physics GPA will match up against the political science majors, relax. If your grades are solid, you have strong academic letters of recommendation, you attended a reputable university, and you have some evidence of writing ability, you will find yourself at no inherent disadvantage in the admission process and may even stand out more. These areas are less subject to grade inflation, and schools make more of an effort to weed people out of the majors. A high GPA in these subjects is a "plus factor" in your applications. I have a client with a 3.9 in Neuroscience and a 165, who has been admitted to ten top fifteen schools, and is currently wait-listed at Harvard.

However, as a science or math major, you may need to make more of an effort to show why law school makes sense for you. If you minor in English or take some political science courses, that can help, and it would also benefit you to seek out letters of recommendation from professors in courses that involve research, writing, and communication skills.

Foreign Languages

Good news: knowing another language shows diversity and, in my mind, is an absolute prerequisite for anyone who hopes to be involved in international law and policy or even in immigration law. And, just think how useful it would be in BigLaw working on international business deals! If you can demonstrate the challenges of your area of study given your background, and if you can show intellectual curiosity, and that knowledge of this language will allow you to serve an underrepresented group as an attorney, then this will go a long way in your applications.

Communication/Journalism

A degree in communication is not seen as particularly challenging or interesting or intellectual on its own. I majored in advertising, so I am not judging. (At least at my alma mater we were required to have two majors, so I also completed a major in history). Hopefully, with a background in communications you can demonstrate that you honed your writing and public-speaking skills. In addition, you can perhaps focus on your advocacy skills.

Ever since November 8, 2016, I've felt strongly that lawyers and journalists will be our heroes during the years when you're most likely reading this book. If you can demonstrate why your participation in journalism is related to your yearning for truth, a willingness and eagerness to investigate, and the importance of facts in drawing conclusions, then I think you can make a clear argument for why this major prepared you for law school and why the same passions that led you to study journalism now lead you to pursue law.

Education

The big question is, why aren't you becoming a teacher? You are trained to be a teacher, and our country needs bright, capable, motivated teachers (arguably much more than we need more lawyers). So why are you applying to law school? It's important to articulate a reason for why you would leave a profession you were trained and certified to enter and one that is valuable and respected. Trust me, I've heard the "I can do more as an advocate for education policy" and "I want to represent families trying to obtain accommodations for their children in the public-school setting." This is very popular with Teach for America participants as well (see Chapter 9).

Obviously, there are traits in teachers that are important for lawyers as well, including patience, diligence, and a desire to serve others, evaluate their needs, and find solutions to their difficulties within a prescribed group of available choices. Teaching is a respected profession where you work hard and try to impact the lives of others in a positive way. This goes a long way with law schools.

Bachelor of Fine Arts (Theater, Dance, Music, Film)

This is tricky, since so much of your training was professional rather than academic, and can be very difficult for professors to explain in terms of academic skills in a letter of recommendation. But when done right, a letter of recommendation can go a long way toward adding credibility to your academic program. It might include how hard you had to work at your discipline and how intense the program is, your personal dedication to self-improvement, as well as your ability to work with others and to take criticism. Hard work and dedication are inherent in these majors. But the other side of the coin is the question of why you are applying to law school—it just seems so obvious and cliché that you got tired of being an out-of-work actor or musician. If you had a double major in an academic subject, you can overcome this presumption a bit, and if you did any academic writing or research, find a way to emphasize it. If you majored in art history or music composition, these show you are a thinking and analytical person—that you can look at something or hear something and make judgments about its origin based on certain clues. Certainly, these skills translate well to law, as are the discipline and commitment required in order to excel.

Recently, I've seen more music industry majors applying to law school. Having an understanding of law is necessary in the music and entertainment business, and undergraduate programs in the music industry often include a study of contracts and copyright law in their music curricula. Even though this may not be the most academic of majors, you probably took some business and law-related classes. It's easy to draw a line between your interest in music and your interest in pursuing law, and as a music major, you can complement experiences and internships on your résumé with examples of legal issues you've dealt with in the real world. It's also easy to connect your reasons to pursue law and why a certain school would appeal to you.

Business/Accounting

Business and law are—and should be—intertwined. After all, lawyers in private practice are all in business (like it or not), and being able to manage a practice is a skill that is often ignored in law school but essential in law practice. Plus, lawyers advise businesses. So, there's no inherent weakness in applying to law school with a major in business. During my years practicing law, I looked at more profit-and-loss statements than Supreme Court opinions, so an understanding of accounting will be pretty darn useful (especially if you plan to manage a law firm one day). An Econ major brings some clout because of the difficulty and intellectual nature of the courses. A business management major at a selective business school is something law schools respect, especially because of the real-world aspect of the education and the teamwork that is often required. These are all good things for law school. However, if your résumé looks more like someone who wants to go into finance or investment banking or real estate, then you need to demonstrate interest in legal issues in your personal statement.

Psychology/Sociology/Identity Studies

These fields are research-based and people-based, and you've probably done some writing, so they are fine majors for applying to law school. Emphasize research and work you've done with faculty on issues relating to policy and law and not just people's inherent inclination toward certain colors and facial features, and you can turn these seemingly soft majors into strengths. Identity studies not only shows intellectual curiosity but also tends to make you sound very idealistic (which works well if you can back up an interest in public-interest law).

How Can I Overcome Perceived Weaknesses in My Major?

Once you know how law schools view your major, think about what you can do to make up for any inherent weaknesses. If you haven't had much writing in your curriculum, try writing for the school paper, for a blog, or becoming a research assistant to a professor. If you've already graduated, emphasize more recent activities that make up for those weaknesses, whether it's writing for your company's blog, drafting reports or business proposals, or even participation in a hobby or volunteer commitment.

How Law Schools Determine Your Academic Performance

All of your transcripts, post–high school level, need to go to LSAC, except some study abroad programs of short duration (see www.lsac. org/jd/apply/cas-requesting-transcripts.asp for more details). You need to follow the instructions at LSAC.org exactly in order to avoid delays in having your applications processed. Denial won't help you: you can't avoid sending the summer school transcripts from the junior college, even if you took the credits while still in high school. That class you forgot to withdraw from still counts too. If you are still in school, you can send updated transcripts at the end of the next term.

Nontraditional applicants should go ahead and send transcripts as soon as possible to find out how LSAC will calculate their GPA. If you are still in college and applying in the fall, go ahead and send the transcripts you have through your junior year/summer before senior year. Does that mean you can fool around during your senior year? Nope! Law schools will want updated transcripts as the application season progresses and will want to see your final transcripts before you enroll. If you are concerned that you haven't had time to pull your grades up, consider waiting a year and applying to law school after you graduate—taking a year off after college. Then law schools will consider grades from your entire senior year. Also, you can update the schools with new activities and accomplishments throughout your gap year. For more about how to explain aspects of your academic background in your application, see Chapter 7, Explaining Your Weaknesses.

Your LSAC Cumulative GPA May Be Different from Your College GPA

Although your graduating institution may not count grades from a transferring institution in your GPA, LSAC will. As a result, there is no advantage to transferring: you don't get a fresh start or "do-over" with your GPA. Some transfers will be happy about this because their early grades at a less-competitive school will now help boost their GPA. Grades with pluses or minuses may be counted differently by LSAC; repeated courses and pass/fail courses may also change your GPA. For example, if you took a class twice, earning a D and a B, current LSAC policy averages this grade to a C, even if your undergraduate institution erases the D.

When LSAC calculates your UGPA, A+ grades count as 4.33. One of my clients, Lauren, figured this out and added classes where she felt she could earn A+s. She ended up raising her GPA by a tenth of a point.

Once you receive your first bachelor's degree, no more credits will count toward your LSAC GPA. Going for another BA, therefore, will not inflate your GPA.

LSAC will create an Academic Summary Report with your new LSAC Cumulative GPA. It will also show a degree GPA, which represents the credits earned at your graduating institution. Law schools need everyone to start on an even playing field. It wouldn't be fair to people who graduated in three years if you could keep going to college for five years to boost your GPA. Likewise, not everyone has a graduate degree, so your graduate school grades can't be used as an objective factor in your application. Although your advanced degree won't count toward this GPA, schools will consider your performance in a reputable program as evidence of your ability to succeed in law school.

LSAC won't count classes you've taken after you've graduated from college. If you have two bachelor degrees, it's the first one that counts. But if it has been a long time since you attended college, and you are trying to show you are a more serious student now, it can help you to take a class or two at a local college. If you do well, this can help you obtain an academic letter of recommendation.

Check lsac.org if you have questions about what transcripts should be sent to LSAC. Do this early in your application cycle—I usually recommend it as the first task my clients attack. It takes time to order the transcripts, more time for your school(s) to send them, and then even more time for LSAC to receive them and review them. It's better to have these delays while you're working on your application materials than when your application has been submitted and is sitting on a dean's desk, unable to be reviewed because she's waiting for your transcripts. Also, if you neglect to send transcripts that later show up through reference on another transcript, law schools will deem your application incomplete and put it on hold. For international applicants, delays are usually even longer. Plan for this entire process to take three to six weeks. Being on top of it and checking in with LSAC to make sure they receive things, will make the rest of the application process less stressful for you.

Failure to send transcripts is one of the biggest mistakes I see made by law school applicants. By not taking care of sending all transcripts, applicants unnecessarily delay their application and lose out on the benefit of rolling admissions. This is why sending transcripts to LSAC is the first thing I have each of my clients do. It also tells you sooner what your LSAC cumulative GPA is so that you can make realistic assessments about schools that are within reach.

If there were circumstances that interfered with your ability to perform to your potential in college—including working significant hours, trauma, illness, undiagnosed disability, family responsibilities, or otherwise—there are ways to bring this information to the attention of the law schools for consideration in order for them to have a holistic view of your grades and put them in context (see Chapter 7).

Law schools make exceptions on the numbers but not on a wholesale basis. They still need to fill their class with people whose numbers fit what they believe indicate law school success, and exceptions need to be balanced out by other members of the class because law schools feed the data regarding their students to LSAC, which in turn produces correlation studies to show who is making it through law school and who is passing the bar on the first try. U.S. News and World Report uses this data to rank law schools, so law schools are extremely numbers-conscious. You need to have an outstanding application to become an exception. How do you know whether you might fall into this category? Read on.

Top-ranked schools will be less forgiving and will be looking for that high overall GPA, no matter your major or circumstances. As you go through this process, it's very important to cultivate resources you can trust. There is so much information out there in the Internet universe, but it's important to evaluate who is giving the advice. Also, it's important to remember that not all situations are universal: the right advice for someone targeting Harvard Law is not necessarily the right advice for someone hoping to go to their neighborhood law school, part-time, while supporting a family. Most schools take your GPA (your LSAC Cumulative GPA) and highest LSAT score (to be discussed in Chapter 4) and assign an index number to your file according to a formula they use to determine who is likely to succeed at their law school. Some schools simply use 25th and 75th percentile numbers as a starting point for initial file categorization. The categorization is based on previous students at that school and how they fared academically and on the bar exam during their first try. The way these formulas are used is not shared with applicants; I'm sharing it here to show you how a file is initially reviewed based on the numbers alone. Your file will be put into one of three piles, basically: Presumptive Admit, Presumptive Deny, and Committee (for the files that are somewhere in between). All of the files are read by someone.

Schools also consider your GPA subjectively based on a number of factors:

- quality of undergraduate school and its students;
- how you performed compared to your peers;
- difficulty of major/changing majors;
- upward trend in grades;
- whether your grades are recent or whether they reflect a younger version of yourself;
- performance in a graduate school program;
- excellent academic letters of recommendation;
- whether you wrote a thesis;
- obstacles you faced as a student; and
- any explanations you provide to explain a period of less impressive grades.

By the time you're reading this, it's probably too late to change which college you attended. So, I share this information not to make you feel bad about your choice but to help you understand how law schools will evaluate you compared to other applicants. The biggest "plus factor" of going to a quality undergrad school is that you are, presumably, competing against a high caliber of student and being taught and graded by highly qualified faculty. The demands and expectations will be higher, so your ability to perform under these conditions, and be competitive, is given weight. This is why a 3.8 from Johns Hopkins or Dartmouth counts more than a 3.8 from the University of Florida or Loyola Marymount. Therefore, someone with these grades from Dartmouth and a 158 will get into a better school (all other factors being equal) than someone with the same LSAT score who went to the University of Florida.

If you began at a community or junior college, law schools may discount high grades there, but if you maintain those grades at the four-year university to which you transferred, law schools will give those grades a lot of weight. If your grades stayed strong after transferring, showing you fared well against students who were admitted as freshmen, this carries weight. If you transferred many times over several years and your grades were inconsistent, it will be important to show an upward trend.

If you attended college while in the military, online courses are understandable. But if you attended Kaplan University or another for-profit institution, law schools know that grades are inflated and top law schools will discount your performance. Like the transfer from community college described above, your reasons for getting an online education might save you. I have seen some people write very effective explanations for why they had to attend school online and why it was actually quite rigorous because of the accountability it requires. It's important to keep in mind that regional law schools are more likely to accept you than top law schools.

Factors that Impact Your GPA

Law schools look favorably on people who consistently improve, understanding that some are late bloomers as they go through college. However, at top-ten law schools, you need to be consistently strong all around. Impressive grades throughout your education are essential, and a lackluster undergraduate GPA can probably be overlooked at this level only if there is significant graduate-level academic work or a very credible reason for a period of poor academic performance (an injury or illness that was resolved, etc.). A strong LSAT score can also balance out a weak undergraduate GPA!

By the way, if you suffered a hardship, like the loss of a parent, during college and *still* graduated with a 3.9, that's something that will greatly impress law schools. It underscores your ability to show resilience and to work well under traumatic circumstances. If, in another case, you've lost a parent and that meant you had to work more hours to support your younger siblings financially, which in turn negatively impacted your grades, this *too* impresses law schools. The difference between these two cases is that the first person can get away with a lower LSAT score, and the second person will need the LSAT score to show that his or her grades aren't indicative of the person's future potential.

If your grades are consistently mediocre, it's hard to get into a reach school unless your LSAT score is off the charts for those schools. Some excellence (in subjects related to law or other thoughtful fields) is preferred over consistent mediocrity. Your "Cs" in Calculus, Organic Chemistry, or even Modern Dance will be easily forgiven, but the same grades in History, Political Science, and Religion 101 will not be viewed so charitably. I would rather see Cs and As on a transcript than all Bs; at least then, I can tell when a student excelled and when she was inspired.

If you studied abroad and credit was issued directly from the foreign institution and you studied abroad for a year, then you need to send those transcripts to LSAC. If you really earned the credits through a US institution, then different rules may apply. For more about this, see http://www.lsac.org/jd/applying-to-law-school/cas/requesting-transcripts. "My study abroad grades at Oxford ended up *helping* my undergraduate GPA. I calculated what my Yale + Oxford GPA would be and highlighted it explicitly on my résumé" (Current Harvard Law student).

If your undergraduate degree was obtained from a foreign institution, LSAC will calculate your GPA to be a shocking 0.0. But don't worry, the law schools know to rely on your evaluation reports. The evaluation service through LSAC will determine whether your grades were Superior, Above Average, Average, or Below Average based on what it knows of your undergraduate institution.

If you attended a school within the United States that does not give grades, your GPA will also be shown as 0.0. Your transcripts of your professor evaluations will be sent to the schools. If you have studied only in a language other than English, you are probably going to need to take the TOEFL, and you are going to need to work on the writing-sample portion of the LSAT because law schools will be reading it to check your fluency under pressure. Many universities in Asia rank students, and this is helpful and persuasive to law schools. Law schools also understand that many other countries do not have grade inflation, and this can work in your favor.

Key Takeaways

- Send all transcripts to LSAC ASAP.
- Understand your cumulative UGPA and how it may differ from your college GPA.
- Consider whether to explain certain factors regarding your major, undergraduate school, or performance.

CHAPTER 4

TAKING THE LSAT

You need to take the LSAT to apply to law school. Although a couple of law schools are experimenting with accepting the GRE as an alternative to the LSAT, and more may choose to do so following the printing of this book, the LSAT is still the ruler of this universe.

The LSAT is currently offered four times each year (February, June, September or October, and December). However, as mentioned earlier, the LSAT will be given six times per year in 2018-2019 and may be offered more regularly after that point. The LSAC is currently considering offering the test in a digital form and more frequently throughout the year, but as of the date of this publication, these are the available options.

You need to register for the LSAT in advance. To register for the LSAT go to www.lsac.org/jd/lsat/lsat-registration-methods.asp. Keep an eye out for changing policies at LSAC that override the information in this book. For example, when I sent this book for its first "final" editing, the rule was still that you could take the test only three times in a two-year period. However, as of May 2017, LSAC is removing this restriction.

This change in policy will be helpful to those whose first three scores fail to reflect their abilities on the exam. It will relieve some pressure on those taking the exam for the third time and help those who suffer from severe testing anxiety. However, it will also mean that people spend more money on the LSAT, will be more likely to take it without preparing adequately, and will chase "goal" scores without a meaningful difference in the outcome of their application decisions. Remember that law schools will still report the highest of multiple scores for rankings purposes, but can see all of your scores within five years of when you apply.

There are three major questions that you need the answers to, all of which will be addressed at length in this chapter:

1. What is the LSAT?
2. When should you take it?
3. How should you prepare for it?

THIS IS NOT A TEST YOU CAN TAKE BLIND OR COLD. See how I put that in ALL CAPS? I'm not freaking kidding. A former client who gave me feedback on an early draft of this book specifically requested that I include "an extra super-sized dose of Ann Levine Brutal Honest ™" (his phrasing and emphasis, not mine). I hope this fulfills his request sufficiently. Planning to take the test just to see what happens? Big Mistake. Huge. (Most of you are too young to understand the *Pretty Woman* reference here but indulge me anyway). The LSAT is important. It's not everything, but it counts for a hell of a lot. Don't mess around: it is three or six months of preparation that has a huge part of determining where you will go to law school *and* how much you will pay for your law degree. You might also surprise yourself and really grow to like the challenges presented in the test. One of my clients who scored in the 170s told me, "It really challenges the way that you think, and it's honestly fun to figure out a tough logic game." YOU SHOULD *PLAN* TO TAKE THE LSAT ONCE AND DO IT RIGHT. Make one plan and commit to it. If it doesn't work out because life gets in the way or you have a bad test day, it's perfectly acceptable to take the LSAT again. And again. And again.

What Is the LSAT and What Does It Test?

The LSAT score range is between 120 and 180. There are five sections on the LSAT, but only three types of sections because one will be experimental and not graded, and one section is given twice. There is no math on the LSAT. The LSAT is an aptitude test, not one based on memorization of facts. It requires preparation to learn the question types and to develop the skills being tested. To assist me in this chapter (since mastery of the LSAT is beyond my expertise regarding how to get into law school), I've called upon five LSAT experts:

1. Nathan Fox is a graduate of UC Hastings Law School and the author of *Cheating the LSAT*. He is an LSAT teacher in San Francisco and Los Angeles. His website is www.foxtestprep.com.
2. Ben Olsen is the founder of Strategy Prep (www.strategyprep.com), an LSAT-preparation company in Washington, DC. Before starting Strategy, Ben earned his JD from George Washington University. (Together, Nathan and Ben offer LSAT advice on the ThinkingLSAT podcast).
3. John Rood is President of Next Step Test Prep (www.nextsteptest-prep.com), an Internet-based private tutoring company.
4. Dave Killoran is the CEO of PowerScore and author of the PowerScore Bibles series of LSAT prep books.

For ease of reference, I'll refer to them each by first name throughout this chapter.

What Is the LSAT and Why Do I Have to Take It?

"Lawyers are gladiators who do battle with words. As such, the LSAT primarily tests your command of the English language. Reading and vocabulary are at a premium, just like they will be in law school and throughout your legal career. The test is comprised of three different types of sections: (a) Logical Reasoning sections ask you to support, attack, or analyze short arguments; (b) Reading Comprehension sections ask you to read long, dense passages and then answer questions about what you've read; and (c) Analytical Reasoning sections, also known as Logic Games, ask you to solve puzzles," says Nathan.

How Much Time Should You Set Aside for Studying?

Plan to study for at least three months and usually closer to four or five depending on your natural abilities on standardized tests and the other commitments you may have. Some students need as much as a year to get the score that represents the best of their abilities. "I prefer that students study less per day, for a longer period of time. I don't even like the idea of 'intensive' study. I think it's more efficient and more civilized to chip away at it slowly. Students can make an amazing amount of progress in just an hour a day," says Nathan.

"I'd aim to do one to two hours per day, five or six days per week, with a couple more hours on the weekend so that you can take—and review—a full-length practice test. More studying can certainly help and might be necessary, but many test takers can burn out. Set a reasonable goal, and only do more when you have the time and want to study. In other words, quantity is great, but quality is better. Make the most of the time you have," says Ben.

One of my former clients, who was working while preparing for the LSAT, advises, "Depending on how time consuming your job is, you should expect to spend every night after work and every weekend studying for the LSAT. Be smart about planning work/life schedule around that time."

"Part of what the LSAT tests is your ability to put your nose to the grindstone. You'll certainly have to do this as a law student, and even more in legal practice, so you may as well start now. One way the LSAC tests your ability to work hard is by making their old tests available. There are no secrets on the LSAT. The questions change from test to test, but only superficially—the same concepts are tested over and over. Every student is different, but I recommend that students complete five full-length practice tests at an absolute minimum," advises Nathan.

"I always advise people to take eight to ten practice tests at a minimum and to be careful not to use all the recent tests just in case you end up having to retake the test—I don't want you to run out of preparation materials that you haven't seen before, " says Dave.

Should I Take an LSAT Prep Class?

There are many kinds of prep courses available for the LSAT, both online and in person. Sometimes people tell me they plan to study on their own for a few months then take a practice test, but I actually believe the reverse order is a better plan so that you can learn good strategies and avoid wasting your time and cultivating bad habits. If you live in a metropolitan area, there are probably good LSAT teachers nearby. However, if you live in a remote area, you will have less choice, so an online option may be better because you'll have access to a better teacher. Online classes may also benefit you if it would be a long commute to the class and if your work schedule would make attendance difficult. If you aren't able to attend with minimal effort, you probably will miss classes and not get the same benefit from the course.

"Look for two things: good materials and a great instructor. The materials part is easy; as long as you're using real LSAT questions, you're off to a good start. Finding a great instructor is harder. Most LSAT teachers do the job only temporarily, picking up some quick cash while waiting for their own legal careers to begin. If you can, try to find a teacher who has fallen in love with teaching the LSAT and decided to make a career of it. Start with Yelp.com to see if there's a highly rated LSAT provider in your area. At a minimum, you should see if you can speak to your actual instructor before plunking down $1,000 or more on a class. The big test prep companies have a mix of good, fair, and poor instructors, with a wide variety of training and experience. Ask how many classes your teacher has previously taught, and ask if you can speak to a former student of that instructor," advises Nathan.

"Ask yourself how you like to learn and what type of structure and environment helps you perform your best. If you know you won't get the work done without being forced into doing it, then a prep course is attractive because it creates structure and prompts you to stay active and engaged. If other people distract you while learning, then maybe you need to self-study or work directly with a tutor. Analyze your own preferences and then determine which of the different preparation options matches those," says Dave.

Whatever you choose to do for LSAT prep, choose wisely. If you're going to take a class, look for one that is more about success and the talents of the teacher than having the biggest marketing budget. Ask around in your areas and read reviews online. And, whatever you do, give it your full attention. "I took Ben's hundred-hour class, and I felt like the biggest impediment to my classmates' success was the fact that they were constantly on their phones during class. As a result, they missed key information and an opportunity to practice the mindfulness that is integral to performing well on the LSAT," said one of my clients.

Nathan sees this all the time: "It always blows me away how many people will pay for a class and either miss classes or show up ill-prepared. Is that your plan for law school? For legal practice? I know a lot of lawyers, and they don't behave that way."

Additional options for LSAT preparation are coming down the pipeline, and some may actually tailor your study plan according to your performance on an initial diagnostic exam, according to Matt Sherman, founder of Metamorphosis Prep. These online options may be priced on a monthly subscription as opposed to in a larger up-front fee. "Customized, interactive, and self-paced curricula will incorporate teaching methodologies we know are effective but aren't currently being used, such as student-directed learning, appropriate challenges targeted to current abilities which are identified through adaptive settings, and spiraled review of previous topics." says Matt.

What Are Things To Be Wary of in an LSAT Prep Course?

"Avoid at all costs companies that don't use real LSAT questions as the basis for their course or materials. And, attempt to try before you buy: familiarize yourself with a company's techniques/practices via inexpensive publications or sample videos or interactions with staff. Additionally, read closely to see what kind of live/personalized assistance you'll receive, whether in class with live instructors or out of class with additional support (like hotline, e-mail assistance, and forum). LSAT preparation as a whole is far better today than it was a decade ago, but there are still distinct differences in how companies help prepare students, and so you want to make sure you are making the right choice for your needs," says Dave.

Ben issues a warning: "Don't think that it will be easy. The success stories you read online are probably true, but the students who wrote those stories probably worked really hard. The key to making the most of any course is to plan on doing a ton of homework outside of class."

Self-Study: Alone but Not Lonely

If you're going to study on your own, then listen to podcasts (like The Thinking LSAT) and follow a study schedule (like the one from Next Step Test Prep, included in the Appendix). "Self-studying has really risen in popularity over the past several years, and I think that has a lot to do with not only the quality of the books out there, but also the other resources that can be used by self-studiers to form a cohesive preparation approach," says Dave. For example, the PowerScore Self-Study Site (http://students.powerscore.com/self-study/index.cfm) offers students a set of free LSAT study plans based on the *LSAT Bibles* and *Workbooks* plus the ability to score every practice test they take. "Those tools then connect to our LSAT forum (https://forum.powerscore.com/lsat), where students can get free advice, including written and video explanations to every single LSAT question. When all these resources are combined, they cover every part of the preparation process and allow students to study on their own without feeling like they are studying alone," said Dave.

Consider finding a study partner. Even if one of you is more adept with the material, that person will learn through teaching the material. And even just making the time to meet someone helps carve out dedicated time in your schedule and keeps you committed. It's harder to bail on someone else.

Choosing an LSAT Tutor

A private tutor is a great way to supplement a prep course or self-study. When comparing tutors, take the time to interview them and to check references or read reviews. Use that time not only to look at a few questions so you get a sense of the style and knowledge of the tutor, but also to examine how well you two get along. "Do you like him or her personally? Does his or her style match yours? If the two of you don't mesh during this preliminary meeting, things won't magically get better as time passes. And don't hesitate to ask to speak to another tutor if you don't like the one you are talking to. Good companies understand that not everyone gets along perfectly, and they should quickly and happily arrange for you to chat with someone new," says Dave.

"Talk to the tutor on the telephone or schedule a one-hour preliminary tutoring session to see what kind of rapport you have. Many people can master the LSAT, but far fewer can help someone else master it. Ask yourself: 'Is this person going to motivate me to study harder? Am I going to look forward to our tutoring sessions? Would I feel comfortable calling this person for extra help when I'm feeling frustrated? Does this person genuinely care about my progress, or is she just doing a job?' Remember that you often get what you pay for when hiring a professional. Hourly rates don't correlate perfectly with teaching ability, but the fact that a tutor is able to command a certain rate in the marketplace usually does indicate skill, experience, and a satisfied client base. If a tutor who charges twice as much gives you three times the improvement, then that's a good value. Finally, ask how much of your tutoring fee goes directly to the tutor. Big prep companies usually take a huge chunk of a tutor's fee off the top. So a tutor whom you're paying $150 per hour might only get $50 of that. Are you getting full value from this arrangement? Or would you be better off paying the entire $150 to an independent tutor, who might be more highly skilled and more deeply invested in your success?" says Nathan (who, admittedly, charges a premium for private tutoring sessions).

Yes, the person you hire should have done well on the LSAT, but more importantly, the person needs to have experience teaching others to do well on the LSAT. Experience in teaching people from different backgrounds is very important, especially for test takers with learning disabilities. According to John, "the worst LSAT instructor is the 178-scorer who just has no idea why a 145 student doesn't understand the material."

Study Tips

Whatever method you choose, Nathan recommends starting by doing a timed section of the test and then reviewing your mistakes and figuring out what techniques you need to avoid those mistakes next time.

"With 80+ practice tests available, students should be doing one timed section of a PT every single day. There's no such thing as an untimed LSAT, so there's no point in 'practicing sound strategies' that might not work once the clock is ticking. I want my students desensitized to the ticking clock, so I encourage them to time themselves every single day, on a single section. Then they can take all the time they need to review and learn from their mistakes," says Nathan.

"The most common mistake students make is going too fast. The hardest questions are at the end of each section, and there's no penalty for guessing. You need to focus on *accuracy* at the beginning of each section. If you're struggling to understand the earlier questions, you're not going to get the later ones right anyway. So instead of racing against the clock, you need to calmly answer the question in front of you correctly and then move on to the next one. You can always guess at the end of the section on any questions you don't complete," says Nathan.

One of my clients (who scored a 177 on his second attempt) offers this advice: "The LSAT is more like an athletic competition, such as a tennis match, than it is a traditional academic exam. It's a test of mental fitness and skill. So as the exam approaches, it's important to be well rested and mentally fresh and to resist the urge to overstudy and tire oneself out. During the exam, there are certain factors you cannot control, such as the type of logic games and the order of sections, but there are many factors you can control. As you prepare, be thoughtful about the factors in your control. When I took the LSAT, I knew exactly when I would go to bed the night before, what I'd do if I had trouble sleeping, when I'd wake up the morning of the exam, what I'd eat for breakfast, how I'd get to the test center and how long it'd take me to get there, what clothes to wear, what I'd eat during the break, what my test room looked like, and where the clock was situated in the room."

How Much Can Someone Expect to Improve from an Initial Diagnostic Score?

I get phone calls all the time from people who are panicking after taking their first practice test and score in the 140s. "How much you improve depends largely on how much effort you put into practicing. But assuming you work hard, almost everyone can go up five points. About half can go up eight to twelve points. And some can go up fifteen points or more.

How much you improve also depends on where you start. Going from 152 to 162, for example, is usually easier than going from 162 to 172. In general, the hill gets steeper as you go up," says Ben.

It can be harder to improve on Reading Comprehension (since that's not a new skill) than on Logic Games, according to Nathan. "The easiest student to help improve is the one who walks in with a 162 as a starting score but has no clue on the Logic Games. This student will almost always end up in the 170s, given enough time."

Do You Really Have the Potential to Score in the 170+ Range?

"When someone who has never seen an LSAT before scores 160 or higher on a first practice test, that person has a very good chance of hitting 170. That said, I've seen many students who have scored lower than that on their first LSAT and end up breaking 170. I've seen a few students who started in the 140s reach 170. That's rare, so don't plan on it. But a big part of their success was persistence. Even though they didn't reach their goal in the typical two or three months many students take to prepare, they worked their way up to the mid-150s, and then worked their way to the mid-160s, and then worked their way up over 170," according to Ben.

When to Take the LSAT

Now that you've heard from the LSAT exam experts, and you're getting an understanding of how much time you'll need to prepare for the test, let's talk about how the LSAT fits into your law school application strategy. For example, choosing a test date is part of your admission strategy. If you are a junior in college planning to attend law school immediately after college graduation, you should plan to take the LSAT either in June after your junior year or in September of your senior year (giving you a chance to study for it over the summer). For June, you'd be studying while still in school, which can be stressful, but if it doesn't go well, you can retake the test in September and still apply very early in the admission cycle.

If you are a senior in college planning to take a year off before law school, the September LSAT lets you spend the summer after graduation focusing on the test. Your backup date will be December, which is still timely for the same admission cycle. (Remember that it takes approximately three to four weeks for scores to be released after the test date).

At some point during the lifecycle of this book, it's likely that the LSAT format will change to allow for it to be taken out of the dark ages and given digitally; this is already being tested at LSAC. When this happens, applicants will have more flexibility in deciding when to take the exam. For now, however, we are stuck with planning in advance when to take the test.

Parting Thoughts on the LSAT

This test is incredibly important. It's not everything, and you shouldn't put your whole life on hold for it, or despair if you put in the preparation and it turns out you're just not a fabulous standardized test taker, but it does count for a hell of a lot. Don't mess around: it is three or six months of preparation that largely determines where you will go to law school *and* how much you will pay for your law degree.

Here are some additional LSAT tips:

1. Sign up early. Otherwise, you may not get a testing location that is convenient for you.
2. If you struggle with standardized tests, don't study on your own.
3. Study amid chaos. One of my favorite former clients (who signed up to work with me after reading the first version of this book and who actually did so without even calling me first—crazy guy!) says, "I took tests cold, hot, indoors, outdoors, in Starbucks, in sports bars from 10:00 p.m. to 2:00 a.m., on a train, on a plane, and on a rural Mexican bus (really!). My Harvard friend, meanwhile, did all of the above plus at least one in a walk-in freezer. That's why she's at Harvard, and I'm not, I guess. Everybody has a story about how they would have done better if not for [some distraction] on test day. But *we* don't, and for that I'm thankful." This client is now a graduate of NYU Law.

4. If you're not ready for the LSAT, don't take it. If you feel unprepared, ill, or distracted, trust your instincts. You can now withdraw up until twenty-four hours until the start time and nothing shows up on your LSAT record.

5. Show up for the test. This means knowing *how* to show up. Read the instructions; know what you can't bring and what you can. That watch you've been using to time yourself during LSAT practice exams for the last six months? You might be banned from bringing it in, and that could cause you major anxiety. Be prepared. Know how to find the room/testing center. Know where to park. Be prepared to wait an hour or two longer than expected; delays in getting started are common. If it is within your control, avoid sitting by the proctor (who will be—without exception—talkative and clueless) or by the door or other high-traffic areas where panicking test takers will be running on the way to the bathroom.

6. It's okay to take the LSAT again. No matter how well prepared you might feel for the LSAT, crazy things happen on test day. You may decide to cancel your score or wait for your score and then decide whether to retake the exam. Although they will see all of your reported scores within a five-year period, law schools have every incentive to place the greatest weight on your highest score. This is what they report to the ABA and for rankings purposes. However, if you have a big difference between your scores, it might raise eyebrows, so you will want to explain what was going on in your application (see Chapter 7, Explaining Your Weaknesses). That weakness is overridden, however, by the fact that you—hopefully—received a higher score on the next exam. The other possible downsides of retaking the test are (1) the additional time spent studying, (2) the cost of additional preparation/taking the exam again, (3) the delay in getting your applications submitted/reviewed, and (4) the possibility that you might have to explain to a law school why your score decreased the second time. Schools that say they average multiple LSAT scores are still inclined to take the higher score, especially if you

provide a good explanation for why the lower score shouldn't be held against you.

It's okay to cancel your LSAT score after the fact and can even show good judgment to do so. You have six days after the LSAT to cancel a score in writing. If you completely screwed up by leaving an entire section blank, misbubbled the last six questions, or became violently ill in the middle of the exam, you should probably cancel. Other reasons for canceling may include significant (nearly unbearable) distractions in the testing center or if you already have an LSAT score that you believe is higher than what you likely earned on this test. Many of my clients know exactly that a certain game or reading passage threw them, but that otherwise they performed within their anticipated range. I often tell them not to cancel in this situation (if it is their first time taking the LSAT) because it's likely that something would throw them on any other LSAT examination as well. I've never had someone say to me that they took the perfect LSAT that hit all of their strengths, only had games they had seen before, experienced the best-possible testing conditions, with quiet neighbors, and enjoyed eight hours of sleep the night before the test. No one experiences perfect conditions (for the LSAT or for anything else in life). I always get a lot of phone calls on those four days a year when the LSAT is given and within an hour of when people are leaving the testing center—thank goodness not all from the same time zone. Everyone wants to know whether they should cancel. I listen closely, let them vent, and then I tell them to call me in twenty-four or forty-eight hours. There is a reason you have six days to consider this decision—you should not be making it when you are stressed or exhausted. Go home after the test. Close the door. Wait a day before logging onto a discussion forum to see what other people thought of the test. Watch Netflix, eat comfort food, and go to sleep. Wake up the next day, work out, and *then* decide. If you still really aren't sure which section was the experimental or what you were supposed to do with the unicorn game (I made this up; don't Google "unicorn LSAT game"—though feel free to Google "dinosaur game" for agonized LSAT memories), then start reading blogs by LSAT teachers and consider looking at the forums to help you determine whether your instincts are correct. But don't make any decisions until you've slept on it. You don't get bonus points for canceling before anyone else. You get bonus points for good decision-making.

The Truth About Very Low LSAT Scores

This is, unfortunately, the most popular topic on my blog and has been since I initially posted about it in 2007. While I do have testimonials on my website from people who received a 150 LSAT and got into top thirty schools, people who fall into this category are few and far between. Moreover, it should be understood that I hand-select these clients because I see that there is something in their backgrounds that top schools will value, whether it's a significant family obstacle overcome, military experience, and/or financial hardship.

When someone with a history of LSAT scores in the low 140s calls me, I am very clear with them about whether their expectations are reasonable. And, to be honest, I turn away those who I feel are unrealistic in terms of where they hope to attend given their credentials. When people fill out a contact form on my website and have an LSAT score in the mid-140s or lower and are hoping for my help, I am honest with them that there is not a lot I can do to help them get into law school, except in very rare circumstances. (If this happened to you, and you filled out a contact form on my website and I said I couldn't help until your score improved, I hope you'll understand where I'm coming from—I won't take your money if I don't feel I can help you reach your goals).

If your LSAT score is in the 140s or lower, you need to spend some time looking at the 25th percentile LSAT scores for the schools you were hoping to attend. How do you find this information? See https://officialguide.lsac.org/release/OfficialGuide_Default.aspx.

If that number is more than ten points higher than your LSAT score, please be realistic that your chances of admission are slim to none (especially if your GPA is also below the 25th percentile for that school).

That's all there is to it—no sugar coating. I have had clients whose LSAT scores are in the low 150s admitted to very respectable law schools, sometimes even in the top twenty. However, in every case there were both (1) a *summa cum laude*/valedictorian/3.9 academic background and (2) one or more significant obstacles overcome, military service or other second-career applicants with very interesting backgrounds and accomplishments.

If you have a low LSAT score, you have three choices:

1. Retake the LSAT and improve your score by doing something differently than you did the first or second time, which may include spending more time preparing and/or trying a new preparation method. For international applicants, it might include spending more time on English-reading fluency, speed, and comprehension. Don't expect the same behavior to bring about different results. If you do plan to retake the LSAT, only do so if you're willing to invest the time and money necessary to really improve the outcome. Think long and hard about whether you could improve your score by increasing preparation time or changing your preparation methods and whether you're willing to do what it will take. If so, then try again. If not, reconsider your goals.

2. Be more flexible in your list of law schools by including schools that do take people with your numbers. If a school never takes anyone with your numbers, then they won't take you—no matter how amazing your personal statement and letters of recommendation may be.

3. Rethink your plans to attend law school. After all, if you have a 2.3 GPA and a 138 LSAT, you—unfortunately—are very unlikely to be able to make it through law school and pass the bar exam after graduation. So making this decision now, before you've invested three years and $150,000, could be the smartest thing you do. This is especially true for those of you harboring a "dream" of becoming a lawyer but who do not have a lot of practical experience in a legal environment and therefore may not have a clear understanding of the profession and its demands. Law school is not the only way to make a difference in this world.

If you have a high 140s LSAT with a GPA of 3.5 or higher and no arrests or discipline issues, then you will probably be admitted to a law school. If you have a disability, but LSAC refused accommodations on the LSAT, writing a persuasive addendum can help. This is also true if you have a history of underperformance on standardized tests (see Chapter 7, Explaining Your Weaknesses).

What about Conditional Acceptance Programs?

There are schools that will offer you the privilege of paying to take a summer course or two with the incentive that participants who earn a certain grade will be admitted to the fall entering class. These programs are sometimes referred to as "AAMPLE" programs. Sometimes, conditional programs are online or on campus. If your LSAT score isn't an accurate predictor of future academic success, this may be your best and only option. But there is no guarantee of acceptance and, before you commit to any programs, ask about the number of people admitted during previous sessions and whether those people went on to graduate once enrolled as law students. For a list of law schools with conditional acceptance programs, see http://www.lsac.org/jd/pdfs/conditional-admission-programs.pdf.

Applying for Accommodations

If you believe you may be entitled to accommodations because of a disability, you should absolutely apply for them. Be aware that you are by no means guaranteed to get what you request or anything at all. You are most likely to obtain accommodations if you have a history of receiving them in other educational environments. Follow directions on the LSAC website regarding how recent your documentation must be, whether you should submit evidence of prior accommodations and what type of documentation is needed. The requirements vary depending on the underlying disability. It often takes time to get copies of files, so start this process early to avoid a delay in review. There are deadlines for the submission of documentation and missing those will put you in a tough position of deciding to take the LSAT without accommodations or wait for the next administration of the exam. Ignore those who say that you should not apply for accommodations because it will prejudice your application. This is largely based on a former policy where people who took the LSAT with accommodations were given score reports that marked that an accommodation was provided. This is no longer the case. What will jeopardize your application is a low score.

Key Takeaways

- Plan ahead to choose an LSAT date.
- Make a study plan and schedule.
- Take at least five full-length timed practice tests.
- You can take the test three times in a two-year period.
- Schools count the highest of multiple scores.

CHAPTER 5

LETTERS OF RECOMMENDATION

What Is the Purpose of a Letter of Recommendation?

The people writing your letters of recommendation (LORs) are the only people who get to speak in your application other than you. This is the chance for someone to discuss your dedication, seriousness, intellectual curiosity, research and writing skills, communication skills, teamwork, presentation skills, and leadership in a way that you cannot without sounding arrogant. The best LORs are written by someone *whom the reader will trust.*

When selecting people (at least two, preferably three, and perhaps four for some schools), remember that it's not *who* you know, it's *how you know them* and what they can say about you that is meaningful to law schools. The best LOR is the (strong) academic letter. A detailed letter from a professor outlining the rigor of the class(es) you took and how you excelled in them, describing your intellectual curiosity, writing and research skills, presentation skills and/or teamwork and problem-solving skills is the best tool for law schools that are trying to ascertain whether you will make it through a rigorous law school curriculum. This is true whether you were a strong student at an elite university or a mediocre student at any school. For example, a strong academic letter can show that you are more than just a strong GPA—that you actually care about what you study, contribute meaningfully, and you are not just doing what's necessary to earn your A.

Professors can discuss that you went above and beyond the required reading, wrote a truly insightful paper that you later turned into a thesis topic, that you came by office hours to engage in the subject matter, that you worked well with others and listened to their ideas, and that you contributed in a meaningful and appropriate way in class. A professor can also add something to the effect of "Rami compares with students whom I have had who went on to attend Stanford Law and the University of Chicago School of Law," or "Noam is in the top 5 percent of students whom I have taught over my twenty-plus-year career at three major universities."

A great academic letter can attest to the fact that you're a better student than your overall GPA might predict. For example, a professor can highlight that you excel in classes that require the same skills you will need to succeed in law school, particularly in the areas of intellectual curiosity, research, writing, and interpersonal communication. Highlighting areas where you excel can bolster any addendum you may write to explain your poor pre-med grades and show that you are engaged in your studies and that you took school more seriously than law schools might assume from your GPA.

People who attend large public schools often have a hard time getting an academic letter, even if they were good students. But remember, a teaching assistant who led a discussion group, who held office hours that you attended, and who graded your work can absolutely write a meaningful letter on your behalf. However, be sure the person will write you a strong letter. Always ask, "Do you feel you could write a strong letter on my behalf?" This will give professors an escape in the event that the teacher actually doesn't think you're as great as you think he or she thinks you are. "Most professors are more observant than you think they are. As such, keep in mind that how you act in class may not go unnoticed. When a professor sees you texting or using your laptop inappropriately, arriving late without a good excuse, or missing class, that behavior may make an unfavorable impression," says Ronald Den Otter, a prelaw advisor at Cal Poly San Luis Obispo.

The prestige of the professor is not nearly as important as what he or she can say about you that is meaningful. What is meaningful?

- A description of the rigor of the course taken with the professor, including the kind of work that is required (essays, exams, research papers, group projects, etc.).

- How you stood out, contributed to classroom discussion, sought out office hours—examples that show you are a serious student who is engaged in coursework, rather than simply showing up and doing the minimum required to get a certain grade.
- An evaluation of your performance on written assignments.
- A comparison between you and other students the professor has taught you went on to law school (or even a certain level of law school).
- It is not helpful for a professor's LOR to recount achievements or things that he or she could not have known about you firsthand. Those things can go on your resume, so that the law schools will know about these accomplishments from other parts of your application.

What If I Don't Have a Professor to Write a Letter?

If you've been out of school for a while or you're a transfer student who hasn't had the opportunity to get to know professors at your new school or you've been on study abroad or simply don't have a relationship with any of your professors, you have other options.

- A supervisor: Someone who is senior to you in a professional environment, who has supervised you in tasks related to those that make for a successful law student and/or attorney, is the next best bet besides a professor. This person should address your skills: things like managerial skills, leadership skills, communication skills, business experience, knowledge of processes of an organization, and an ability to work well with others, or an ability to solve problems proactively and responsibly. Examples of these skills are crucial to the letter's credibility. Of course, asking your supervisor can get sticky if you don't want your current employer to know you are applying to law school. If you feel comfortable having your supervisor write a letter for you, you should let him or her know that an LOR for law school is a different beast than the often-generic, overly broad professional reference. See a sample, later in this chapter, that you can give your supervisor, and feel free to share the tips in this book.

- An internship supervisor: *If* and only if you really did something impressive during your internship. If you did a run-of-the-mill errand-running, coffee-grabbing, document-editing, phone-answering grunt-work internship, it's not likely to yield a very persuasive LOR. If you gave Capitol tours, blech. If you truly helped a constituent solve a significant problem and found the resources he or she needed and advocated the issue to the legislative assistant, who bumped it up to your Congress member, then YES on the LOR. If you were offered paid employment after the end of your internship, that's great—but it can probably be explained sufficiently on your résumé, especially if your internship was in business or marketing or investment banking and might leave people wondering why you would leave. If you worked in a law firm or legal office, and you stayed beyond summer break and ended up supervising other interns, and so on, then I make an exception to the "no internship letter" rule, especially for people who are struggling to obtain academic letters.

- A military supervisor: Your commanding officers write great LORs because they are detailed, usually in bullet-point format, and very straightforward. I love these letters, and they help make your résumé a little more manageable, as details of your responsibilities and the number of tanks you manned/provisions you ordered can be included in the LOR.

- An alternative professor: Take or audit a college or graduate-level course and get to know the professor, even if you're not taking it for credit.

- A professional: Someone at a nonprofit organization where you've contributed a significant amount of time, if the person can speak to your lengthy dedication, motivation to serve this particular organization, and contributions to the organization.

- A colleague: If you have owned your own business or been a freelancer, consider asking a professional you've worked closely with (such as a lawyer or accountant) who can speak to your involvement with sophisticated professional issues.

Who Should I Avoid Asking for an LOR?

I do not want to see LORs from family friends. If you think you're an exception to this rule, you're not. Why am I so insistent about this when your parents swear their friends will write you fabulous letters? It goes back to the purpose a letter needs to fulfill to strengthen your application. The writer is the only person who gets to talk in your application other than *you*. Your letter writer must say things he or she knows about you from personal experience. This is what adds credibility to the things you are saying about yourself in the rest of your application. The content of the letter must be relevant to your law school application; your mom's tennis partner who happens to be a lawyer, judge, or state senator is not in a position to speak to those qualities.

Even if your parents are pressuring you to ask their well-meaning, successful friends for letters, please say "Thanks, but no thanks." That nice judge who went to law school with your mom and who allowed you to "shadow" him for two hours cannot speak to your strengths and assure a law school that you have what it takes to succeed. Why not, you ask? After all, you had a really, truly, absolutely remarkable and wonderful twenty-minute conversation about law school and the practice of law wherein you are convinced you knocked his socks off? Okay, let's imagine what that letter might say:

"As a friend of Shaina's mother for the past twenty-two years, I have heard stories of her progress. I have heard that she has been deeply involved in her sorority and its philanthropic activities. I recently met her for coffee and perceived her to be sincerely interested in the legal profession. I was not surprised to learn that she did well on the LSAT. I am therefore confident she will make an outstanding law student."

Blech. But if this person offers to write you a letter, there may be a way to put this connection to good use in another way. If you have time, you could arrange to work part-time for this person or take a volunteer internship. Or, if you are applying to the law school this person attended, perhaps he or she could make a phone call or send an e-mail on your behalf to one of his or her contacts at the school. Or you could say, "Thank you so much, but I already have my requisite number of letters. Could I take you up on this offer if I am wait-listed? And, perhaps, could I spend a week in your courtroom during my summer break? Or could you introduce me to any lawyers who you think would be good mentors for me as I embark on my career?" (As I discuss in *The Law School Decision Game*, networking is important. Turn this into an opportunity to start building your law career now. Just because you don't want an LOR from someone doesn't mean they have nothing to offer you in terms of expertise, advice, and connections.)

How Should I Ask for an LOR?

You should give someone three to four weeks to write a letter. Professors may require even more lead time, especially during busy times of the academic year. Remember that the person is doing you a favor. If possible, ask in person rather than through e-mail. Go at office hours; don't interrupt the professor on the way in or out of class.

I don't believe in the value of giving a professor your personal statement or résumé to help them write their letter because a letter of rec needs to add something new and shouldn't just read like a canned recitation of your résumé; this will show that the professor really doesn't know you at all and was a bit desperate for material. Instead, offer the professor bullet-point reminders of the work you did in class and things you are hoping he or she will address. If a professor knows about your extracurricular activities firsthand (as advisor to a particular organization) or about your work experience (because he or she recommended you for a particular job on your résumé and/or discussed your experiences at a position with you in a mentor capacity), then these items can be incorporated into an LOR with credibility. If a professor asks you for a copy of your personal statement, provide a "Why Law"–related essay, one that mentions your undergraduate coursework and the career you envision for yourself, rather than the personal statement that you will send with your applications. I recommend this for a few reasons: (1) to avoid having a professor parrot back your personal statement, (2) to avoid delays in obtaining the letter if you are still working on your personal statement, and/or (3) to avoid sharing personal information you may not be comfortable with your professor knowing.

If a professor seems lukewarm or less than enthusiastic about writing a letter or asks you to jump through a lot of hoops before he or she will agree to write the letter, this is a good indication that it might not be a strong letter. Remember, quality over quantity.

What Can I Do While Still in College to Make Sure I Get Good LORs?

Get to know your professors/letter writers: don't just show up one day (or worse, send a random e-mail) asking them to spend time writing an LOR. Cultivate these letters through visits, coffee chats, intellectual discussions, and meetings where you seek advice about your goals and future career. And, of course, taking their classes seriously helps too! If you are in college, visit professors during office hours, try to take more than one class with at least two professors, and offer to help a professor with his or her research interests.

How Many LORs Do I Need?

LSAC will hold up to five letters for five years. Schools usually accept between two and four LORs. When deciding which letters to send to schools, I'd rather have only two letters that are both strong, instead of three letters where the third is mediocre. However, get the letters into LSAC and then decide which you want to submit with each application based on what the school requests.

What Do I Do If They Ask Me to Write My Own LOR?

If someone asks you to prepare an LOR for his or her signature, do not freak out. This is fairly standard practice in the professional world. Here's a brief outline of how to approach it:

> **Paragraph 1**: Outline the writer's experience to build his or her credibility. Provide facts demonstrating the context in which the writer knows you, including his or her supervisory role and the length of time he or she has known you.
> **Paragraph 2**: Provide an overview of your accomplishments and duties.

Paragraphs 3–5: Use factual examples of certain characteristics you would like to highlight. Consider including a time you solved a problem in a professional and diplomatic way, how you demonstrated your writing skills, and/or your willingness to go above and beyond the call of duty. For example, instead of just saying you have communication skills, reference letters or materials you created that were used for internal or external matters or a time you were selected to be part of a more senior team and earned the respect of coworkers and/or senior managers.

Conclusion: State the qualities you bring to law school and why the person highly recommends you for law school admission and that he or she is available to answer questions about your experience and candidacy.

Do I Need Targeted LORs?

You do not need your LORs to be for a specific school. The only reason to do this is if the person writing your letter has graduated from that law school or teaches at that law school. Otherwise, use the same letters for each school.

How Do Letters Get Sent to Each School?

When you submit each application, you will designate the letters that you wish to accompany it. It's okay if the letter hasn't been received yet at LSAC. Your application will still be submitted, and the letter will follow upon receipt. If a school wants two letters, you'll designate which two letters you want sent with that particular application. If a school requires two letters, but allows for more, and you submit the application without all of the letters received by LSAC, the school will move your application into review after receiving two letters—whichever of the two comes in first.

How Long Can Letters Stay on File at LSAC?

LSAC will hold onto your LORs for five years. If you are in college or graduate school and even remotely considering applying to law school at some point, please go ahead and register for LSAC and get LORs that can be held for future use, as it's unlikely that your professors will remember you even a few months beyond graduation. If you're out of college, there is no need to update an academic letter because you wouldn't have taken additional courses with that professor. A work reference, however, from a current employer should be updated and given a more recent date if you apply in a later cycle because that person would have more current information to add to the letter.

Should I Waive My Right to See the Letter?

Yes. This doesn't mean you've never seen it or that it won't be shown to you in the future. It simply means you won't sue LSAC or the law schools to see your letters. And it adds credibility to the letter because it is assumed that people will be more candid if they know you will never lay eyes on its content. If it makes you nervous to waive your rights, then you aren't feeling confident about the strength of the letter and should consider asking someone else to write a letter on your behalf.

Sample LORs

Below are some sample LORs. Please take care to change the language should you show these examples to your recommenders or if you are drafting your own letter for someone else's signature. Law schools recognize the repetitive language, and it is better for people to phrase things in a way that is more natural for them. This is part of creating a credible LOR.

Sample Professor Letter (Enthusiastic)

Dear Law School Admissions Committee:

My name is _____ and I am writing this letter on behalf of _____, and I could not be happier to do so. _____ is one of my three or four best students ever at _____. I was her instructor in three courses: Civil Liberties, Civil Rights, and Introduction to the American Legal System. _____ received an "A" in all of them and was the best student in each of them as well. Several years ago, I handpicked her for an internship with a local law office because I knew that she would make a terrific impression, and I wanted to induce other attorneys to participate in the continuing internship program. Also, I have interacted with her many, many times, both inside and outside of the classroom, including a field trip to law schools and pre-law club meetings. I know her better than just about any undergraduate that I have had as a student during my time here, and I have nothing but nice things to say about her. _____ has multiple talents but, at times, doesn't seem to appreciate how talented she really is, which is part of her charm. Every interaction with her feels genuine, and she is so likable in numerous ways. She has the maturity of a much older person, and I know that she will live up to the high standards of achievement that she has set for herself.

Academically, _____ is also one of the best students that I have ever had. The numbers speak for themselves. She has an undergraduate GPA higher than 3.8 (and there is little or no grade inflation at _____), and I would put her in the top 1 percent of the students that I have taught at five different universities. More importantly, she has the intellectual curiosity and meticulousness of a future law student and lawyer. She reads texts carefully, reflects on what she has read, develops her own interpretations, and defends them effectively—both orally and in writing. Unlike too many undergraduates, she never asked me what I wanted her to do, as if she were supposed to follow a recipe. Instead, she would take the initiative and could be counted on to work on her own with little supervision. In other words, she took responsibility for crafting particular answers to the interpretive or normative questions that she addressed in her written work. She would not just formulate her own view but would also develop an understanding of the various interpretations before judging among them.

The reading in public law classes is always challenging for undergraduates. In my classes, _____ exhibited patience and never jumped to conclusions without adequate evidence. When concepts were difficult, she recognized their difficulty and did not oversimplify them or pretend that she understood them perfectly when she didn't. She never felt that she had to impress me or my colleagues by presenting herself as more knowledgeable than she really was. During her time here at _____, she has always been receptive to constructive criticism. For her, there was always room for a deeper understanding of the material. That is only one of the reasons why she stands out so much, even among our best students. She didn't just care about her grades; she genuinely wanted to develop her academic skills as fully as possible.

_____'s work exhibited the kind of care and attention to detail that one would expect of a law student. I was also impressed with her technical writing ability. I have never had an undergraduate student who wrote graduate school-quality papers before or who was so advanced in her ability to understand difficult legal concepts. The topics that she chose to write on in my public law courses demonstrated surprising theoretical sophistication, and her writing was always clear and concise. Because _____ ran her proposed paper topics by me ahead of time, she could incorporate my suggestions before producing a final draft. As a result, I could not have been more pleased with the quality of her papers, which were a joy to read.

_____'s performance in class, furthermore, was superb. She regularly contributed to each topic that we addressed, stated her views confidently, and treated her classmates with respect. I cannot say enough about the quality of her participation and her attitude toward learning. She always struck me as a student who was willing to go the extra mile to realize her potential. _____ is well-organized, very bright, thoughtful, and highly motivated. It is obvious that her academic ability speaks for itself, but that isn't primarily what makes her the wonderful person who she is. I want to end this letter of recommendation by bringing five main points about _____ to your attention: (1) She is remarkably mature and responsible for someone who is still an undergraduate; (2) She is very open minded, listens carefully, and thinks before speaking; (3) She is not the sort of person who just likes to hear herself talk or takes herself too seriously; (4) For someone who is very smart, she is down-to-earth and avoids the kind of arrogance that is too common among highly educated and successful people; (5) And, most importantly, she has put time and effort into thinking deeply about her decision to go to law school.

For these reasons, coupled with her academic accomplishments and potential, _____ deserves a place in your first-year class. I know that there is a tendency for professors to exaggerate the virtues of their students in writing a letter like this one, but I cannot recommend any student more highly than _____. She will be able to work with others in a manner that brings out the best in everyone and, ultimately, you (we) will be very proud of her professional accomplishments. She is exactly the kind of person who you're looking for when you're selecting a first-year class and expect excellence. If you have any further questions, you can e-mail me at bestprofeva@fmail.com or call me at (555) 555-5555 (cell).

Sincerely,

_____

Sample Professor Letter (The kind you want to avoid)

My name is _____, and I am writing this letter of recommendation on behalf of _____, a student of mine in a summer course ("_____") at _____. I am happy to write such a letter. In my courses, I stress the importance of being able to apply abstract legal principles to new sets of facts, paralleling the kind of judgment that law students and lawyers are supposed to exercise, and to draw subtle distinctions when appropriate. _____ was always prepared for class and pleasant to be around. She regularly contributed to each topic that we addressed, asked decent questions, and stated her views confidently. Her written work wasn't bad, and I appreciated her attitude toward learning. I would put her in the top 50 percent of the undergraduates that I have ever had at the five four-year universities where I have taught. If you have any further questions, you can e-mail me at worstprofeva@fmail.com or call me at (555) 555-55555 (cell).

Sample Internship Letter

I am writing to support _____'s application for law school. As her supervising attorney at South Brooklyn Legal Services this past summer, I can attest to _____'s outstanding research and writing skills as well as her passion for legal services work. Even as an intern, she was a tremendous asset to this office and made a real difference in the lives of the clients on whose cases she worked. As a law student at your university, I know she would contribute more of the same top-quality work I saw from her this summer.

First, in my five years as an attorney in the housing law unit at this office, I can honestly say that I have never had a better experience working with any summer intern. With every assignment I gave her, I could trust that _____ would approach the work conscientiously and diligently and would return with an exceptionally well-researched and well-written work product. In fact, toward the end of the summer, I left _____ almost entirely on her own to handle a case involving wrongful termination of a client's Section 8 subsidy. _____ met with the client to identify the problem and collect relevant documents from her, identified the claims involved, and drafted the federal court complaint and the brief in support of an order to show cause. Her understanding of the issues was so accurate, and her writing so clear, that I barely edited the papers before filing them in court.

Second, it is not only _____'s research and writing skills that are superb. I observed her interactions with clients in settings ranging from court appearances to office appointments to tenant association meetings. Without exception, _____ was compassionate, patient, and professional. Likewise, she was articulate and confident in her interactions with opposing counsel in court.

Finally, I have met very few law students—and indeed, few young attorneys——who are as mature as _____ is in their commitment to legal representation for the poor. She truly believes in the importance of the work and knows how to translate that belief into high-quality advocacy. The attorneys at _____, as well as our clients, benefited enormously from _____'s dedication this past summer. We will be thrilled if she returns to this office as an intern or attorney in the future.

My direct line is (555) 555-5555. Please feel free to call if I can be of any further assistance.

Yours truly,
Attorney's Name
Senior Staff Attorney Housing Law Unit

Key Takeaways

- Choose recommenders whom the law schools will trust.
- Prioritize academic and professional recommendations.
- Avoid asking family friends.
- Letters should include examples of your contributions and accomplishments.

CHAPTER 6

EVALUATING YOUR STRENGTHS

A s a law school admission consultant, I spend considerable time and energy thinking about each of my client's strengths. Almost everyone has something, whether it's evident from their résumés and transcripts or not. Sometimes I have to get people to dig deep and think of themselves as a third party would; often we can't see the interesting parts of our own stories simply because they are our own. In this chapter's discussion of strengths and soft factors, we are leading up to the really big chapter—the one on the Personal Statement. But until you've really thought about your strengths, you're not ready to think about what to write in your personal statement. (Same with your weaknesses, by the way, because you will need to know what you have to counteract in order to make your personal statement effective.)

What Are Soft Factors?

Law schools don't want people who simply go to school and get good grades. They are looking for insights into your character, your interests, your potential for contributing to the world around you. They want to know you have experienced the world through work, extracurricular and volunteer activities, and travel. They want to know you have been exposed to the big, wide world and that you have learned to get along with others. If you don't have any of these things, get them. Seek out diverse learning opportunities and experiences. Law schools want well-rounded applicants.

Therefore, anything outside of your LSAC Cumulative GPA and LSAT score is considered a "soft" factor in the admissions process. These things are strongly taken into account by law school decision makers. However, they are expected; it looks strange when an applicant has nothing to report on a résumé. So having typical internships and activities is the norm, not exceptional. You need these activities, but understand that they are the baseline and not necessarily an exceptional tipping point for your admission into law school.

People (especially parents) often overestimate the value of these experiences. Having one internship with your Congress member or in a district attorney's office is not going to blow anyone away, but it's nice that you showed interest in law. A summer studying abroad is better than staying home, but it isn't going to go a long way in impressing law schools. When a parent calls and tells me that their "child" has "great internships" I usually roll my eyes. But, I still listen for those nuggets of brilliance. I remember rolling my eyes as one mom expounded on her brilliant son attending Rutgers; then she started saying how he was president of the group representing all public universities in New Jersey *and* a Fulbright Scholar, and I was like, "*HELLO!*" (He turned out to be one of my all-time favorite clients and is a recent graduate of the University of Michigan School of Law, and his mom is right—he is brilliant).

Below are some examples of impressive soft factors (juxtaposed with factors that carry less weight in the process).

Student Activities and Leadership

Law schools are looking for people who are committed, who work well with others, who tackle difficult issues, and—above all—who care. Your record of student involvement helps speak to these qualities. Some activities that law schools especially appreciate include

- taking on a leadership role in serving an underrepresented community and/or advocating for a political, policy, human rights, or community issue;
- serving at a high level in student government;
- having multicultural awareness, fluency, and openness;

- becoming involved with a journal or academic publication, for example being executive editor of your undergraduate law or philosophy journal; and
- participating in competitive athletics (more on this, below).

Being a member of Phi Alpha Delta is nice and shows you've been interested in law (particularly if you did not join recently in order to add it to your résumé), but law schools will always, without question, prefer to see in-depth leadership and exploration of your passions over résumé fillers that you think sound good for a law school applicant. Whether it's a cultural organization, student government, athletics, or volunteering, demonstrate leadership, growth, and dedication in your involvements rather than simply collect memberships in a number of different groups. If you use your time in college to explore things that really interest you, no matter how prestigious you feel they look to others, law schools will take notice.

If you are going to focus your undergraduate commitments in a Greek organization, then use this time to develop skills—as treasurer, risk manager, or house manager you will be handling real responsibilities, addressing conflicts, and gaining practical skills. Do not overstate your experiences—all fraternities have public service, so don't give yourself credit for community service unless you've really gone above and beyond to contribute to and/or lead your organization's philanthropic efforts.

If your undergraduate years are behind you, law schools will look to your current professional and personal pursuits. Do you volunteer regularly at the women's shelter or animal shelter? Do you serve as a Court-Appointed Special Advocate or mentor a child through Big Brothers/Big Sisters? Do you volunteer for political campaigns or help clean up beaches on the weekends? Consider what you are doing to serve others and contribute to your community. If your professional and personal commitments preclude such activities, law schools will understand that. But keep in mind that if your work experience is not especially impressive or related to law in some way, your volunteer endeavors can help show that your heart really leans in that direction.

Athletics

Being a Division I (or III for that matter) athlete during college shows dedication, time management, teamwork, and a host of other positive qualities. If you kept your grades up while pursuing athletics, law schools are going to be impressed. If you were heavily involved in a club sport, this can also be a plus factor in your application. A lot of people start out as college athletes and do not stick with it either because of injury, the pressure getting to them, or their grades suffering. I've read a lot of injured athlete stories. If you really used this experience as a turnaround and can truly demonstrate you picked yourself back up, applied your new-found time to your academics (and perhaps to apply your passions toward another extracurricular endeavor), then you can use this as a positive. However, if you haven't participated in your sport for a couple of years and you sort of floundered after, then please do not write a personal statement about being an athlete. I don't want you to sound like a has-been.

If some time has passed since your college years, showing your involvement in sports at the time can be a way to distance yourself from your academic record (assuming it's lackluster). However, this probably shouldn't be addressed in your personal statement; it's more appropriate for an explanation of weaknesses (see Chapter 7).

International Experience

The United States is a microcosm of people from different backgrounds, nationalities, and cultures. Your ability to work within this environment is seen as a plus factor in your application. Back when I was in college, I didn't know anyone who studied abroad. Today, studying abroad is ubiquitous, so by itself I do not consider it a plus factor in your application, especially if you went somewhere that is a popular American tourist destination (London, Melbourne, etc.) where English is spoken. A significant amount of time (not a summer) spent at a school in the United Kingdom under the tutorial system, and achieving excellence in this environment, holds some weight with law schools. If you studied in a foreign language, law schools will be more impressed. If you pursued a few different opportunities to study international issues in various countries, showing dedication to learning different viewpoints on the issues you studied during college, this adds depth to your academic career. Also, if you held an internship or worked while abroad, this can enhance your experience in the eyes of law school decision makers.

Other international experiences that are relevant to your law school application include the following:

- if you lived abroad during a formative period in your life and therefore became fluent in another language and familiar with another culture;
- if you served abroad while in the military;
- if you are an international student coming to the United States to obtain an education; and
- if you are an immigrant to the United States yourself.

International applicants often wonder how much they count as being "diverse." Of course you bring diversity! American institutions need you in order to expose American students to different ideas, cultures, and networks (especially in our current climate of international students choosing to go to Canada and Australia over the United States, fearing changes in our visa policies under the current administration). You bring something interesting and different to the equation. You learned a new language and attended school alongside those who have been speaking English their whole lives—that's impressive. You got yourself a scholarship to boarding school; you sought to improve your own circumstances even without parents pushing you to do so; you majored in English at a Chinese university and excelled at the LSAT all the same—these are all valuable experiences that law schools appreciate. In the past few years, I've had clients from China and South Korea admitted to Harvard Law School. You are at no disadvantage in the process, and your perspective and knowledge benefits the student body at large.

Military Experience

Your time in the military is highly valued by law schools. The longer you served, the more it helps your application. If you attended school while in the military, make sure this is obvious somewhere on your résumé or elsewhere in your applications because it helps explain school choice and attendance patterns if you were deployed, etc. Members of the military do a great job on résumés and LORs—both are really detailed, and accomplishments are quantified and comparable to others. How quickly were you promoted? How many people did you oversee? How much equipment were you responsible for maintaining? These are the kinds of facts that give the reader of your application a sense of your responsibilities. And, in other parts of your application, it may be relevant to use your diversity statement to provide background on why you entered the military, such as circumstances at home, not being able to afford college, etc. Then you might use your personal statement to talk about lessons learned while in the military that led you to law (or to the next step on your résumé, if you are not coming directly from the military to law school). If you are from a country where military service is compulsory, it is still something worth addressing in your application and is an experience that law schools will appreciate. Military applicants should take care to explain their duties and positions in layperson's terms rather than assume the reader will be familiar with wording and abbreviations.

Work Experience

Let me start by going on a tangent about what lawyers really need to be good at. Most of you will be in business as a lawyer. Having business skills, knowing how to make a profit, being good with people—this is all essential to success as a lawyer. Therefore, being able to demonstrate that you have already begun to develop these skills is a huge plus in your application. Having an understanding of how the world works, being able to manage a budget, not being afraid of grunt work, and having a willingness (eagerness!) to work hard are all huge plus factors in a law school application. Working during college shows financial self-reliance and the ability to multitask. However, these skills are not going to override lower LSAT scores and GPAs.

I've had clients with 20+ years as a paralegal, others who have run businesses, founded start-ups, worked in investment banking or at the White House, and even been dentists, philanthropists, engineers, actors, dancers, aestheticians, and poker players. In some cases, your prior career shows your interest in law, but in other cases, you need to show why law school makes sense for you at this time in your life and that you know what you're getting yourself into. But these careers can also show attention to detail, creative problem solving, a willingness to do lowly tasks to pursue a discipline, to spend hours and hours fine-tuning a craft, a capacity for building a practice, a passion for helping others, a practical sense of what has to be done to feed yourself and/or a family, and a sophisticated mind and the ability to make some savvy work in your favor. To create a compelling personal statement, consider what your résumé says about you and how you can make it applicable to law.

It's also important to recognize the difference between assisting in your mom's real-estate practice (where you are absolutely learning all of the skills I just mentioned) and running a new initiative at Google. The first type of work experience is going to be impressive to many law schools, but the second type of work experience is going to get you into a big reach school.

Internships

During the free initial consultation that I offer for my law school admission consulting services, parents will often call, and these parents will often start by telling me that their adult child has had "great internships." These invariably include things like "Semester in DC" programs, interning with a member of Congress (which really just means answering calls and giving tours), or something along these lines. And then they proceed to tell me that the Congressperson will be writing their "child" a fabulous LOR. *Oy.*

Internships are, in fact, different from work experience. You may or may not have been paid (if you were, you should say so on your résumé). These opportunities also vary greatly in terms of exposure they offer to real office operations and substantive decision-making. A lot of people (okay, usually parents) assume that fancy-sounding internships with district attorneys or member of Congress or law firms are incredibly impressive. Yes, it's good to have internships, but it's better to do something you're really passionate about: something different off the beaten path.

Or, conversely, to come back to the same job more than once to show you are handling increased responsibility and you are seen as a more permanent member of the professional team, rather than another pre-law student passing through the office. If you have had two or three internships in quasi-related fields, it shows that you are really exploring a potential career. I like to see that. If you've had two to three internships in totally unrelated fields (public relations, sports, journalism, law, etc.), then it sort of just looks like you don't know what you want to do—you are lacking direction and haven't found your stride yet.

An internship has more credibility if you were later offered a job, if you worked there more than one summer, or if you were in charge of training other interns.

Diversity

Before you read this section, take a deep breath. Some of you do not bring diversity to the table. You need to be okay with this. You can't worry about being at a disadvantage in the law school-admission process because you haven't been disadvantaged in your life. I promise you, diversity alone won't get someone with a 2.3 and 140 LSAT into law school instead of you. And I'm not going to waste time arguing about whether affirmative action is fair; I'm not going to change your mind, and I promise you aren't going to change mine. So let's just stay focused on what you need to know for law school applications.

Here's what counts as diversity in terms of overcoming significant obstacles:

- socioeconomic disadvantage, including growing up in subsidized housing/using food stamps, being in a single-parent household, financial struggles, needing to work from a young age, and/or limited access to support systems;
- experiences as the child of immigrants, such as needing to translate for your parents or attending schools where a significant portion of the population did not come from English-speaking homes;
- experiences with abuse/poverty/tragedy;

- time spent in the foster-care system;
- a limiting disability; and
- discrimination and disadvantage due to race and/or sexual orientation.

The key, however, is in "overcoming" your circumstances. You won't get into law school with a series of excuses in your personal statement making your disadvantages very clear but not your ability to overcome them. After all, what's impressive is that you got yourself that degree despite lack of parental support, learned English as a teenager, and/or contributed to your family's finances while putting yourself through college, and that you have a valuable perspective as a result, one that will help you relate to (perhaps similarly situated) clients as an attorney.

Being fluent in a language other than English is very helpful for an attorney, given the diverse population of our country and the globalization of our daily lives. Understanding what it feels like to be a minority or someone who has been ostracized (e.g., coming of age in post-9/11 America as a Muslim, Pakistani, or Sikh, or living in the Bible Belt and being gay) is another way of demonstrating diversity.

In terms of deciding how to present this information, here are some rules of thumb:

- If most of your overcoming-obstacles story is pre-college, then consider using it for a diversity statement for schools that provide that opportunity.
- If you talk about childhood/teenage experiences in your personal statement, keep it to a minimum, and use it only to provide context for your more recent decisions, experiences, and achievements.
- If finances or sexual assault or a family illness impacted your grades in college, consider sharing that information in an addendum to explain your grades (see Chapter 7).
- Be wary of repeating the same information in each aspect of your application. Law schools will read your application as a whole, so you don't need to mention the same circumstances in different places.

Key Takeaways

- Significant work experience is a plus factor, especially if you can make your knowledge and skillset relevant to the practice of law.
- Overcoming significant obstacles in life shows drive, tenacity, maturity, and a sense of purpose.
- Commitment to causes and organizations that matter to you is a plus factor in your application.

CHAPTER 7

EXPLAINING YOUR WEAKNESSES

When and How Should I Explain a Weakness in My Application?

There are basically two types of weaknesses that may be explained in a law school application. One is mandatory (character and fitness questions, including criminal record, disciplinary infractions, gaps in your education, etc.), and one is meant to provide context to your achievements (LSAT, GPA, disability explanation, etc.). Your explanation of these issues in your application is typically referred to as an "addendum" to your application.

General rules about addenda include the following: they should be brief, factual statements; this is not the time for narrative devices or histrionics. This is the time when you are most like a lawyer: state your facts, provide an argument for why this issue won't plague you during law school or in your legal career, and get out. Sob stories don't work here. Below are some of the topics that arise most often in addenda.

How Do I Explain My Lackluster Grades?

The best excuses for a poor GPA are:

1. working your way through school;
2. changing from a science-based major (from pre-med to pre-law);
3. personal or family trauma; and
4. participation in intercollegiate athletics.

The best way to show that your GPA should not be used to judge your potential to compete in law school is to provide evidence. One approach is to emphasize the courses you have taken which are rigorous and demanded research, writing, and analysis. Strong grades in those types of courses can help the law school to see your potential for academic success.

For example:

1. "For my first two years of college, I worked thirty-five hours per week as a waitress to support myself and my daughter. After I got married, in the fall of 2007, I no longer needed to work more than fifteen hours per week. Beginning that semester and continuing through the rest of college and through my master's degree program, my GPA never fell below a 3.5, and I earned Dean's List honors during my last three semesters of college." (This shows that the circumstances that prevented your early dismal performance have been overcome and that you have proof that you are capable of performing at a higher level than your early grades would indicate.)

2. "As a college freshman, I felt great pressure to follow in my parents' footsteps by becoming a mechanical engineer. However, I struggled in the prerequisite courses because I was not interested in the topics. When I took my first political science class, I felt sincerely engaged in the work and was rewarded with my first A grade in college. After I changed my major to political science, my GPA stayed above a 3.6." (This shows that once you figured out that engineering wasn't for you, you did well in classes that correlate to performance in law school.)

3. "My grades dropped in my junior year because (my father died/I had mononucleosis/my parents lost their jobs). For the next two years, I was commuting home often to (help my family/get medical treatment/work to help pay the mortgage). Therefore, my transcripts do not accurately reflect my academic promise. However, [the problem has now been resolved by X] these issues will not continue to inhibit my academic performance in law school."

4. "For the first three years of college, I spent X hours per week training, practicing, and traveling as a member of the Division 1

tennis team. During a match in March 2010, I injured my shoulder. After that, I was unable to play tennis, and my time was spent in physical therapy. I struggled with depression and motivation after this change in my life but finally rallied to concentrate on school during my last semester. In the Spring of 2012, I earned a 3.7 GPA while taking three 400-level classes, which demonstrates my academic success when I am able to focus on school (which I plan to do in law school)."

If you were a typical eighteen-year-old living away from home for the first time, who was more interested in partying and video games than attending classes, the good news is that you are in good company. If you rallied later in some way that shows maturity and growth, then you'll have a story that works. Did you get a job that showed a level of dedication not evident in your grades? Get involved in a meaningful activity? Those things can help, but it's still a hard hurdle to overcome in an addendum, and it is very important for those of you who fall into this category to draft a really effective addendum. One way to do this might be to showcase your strengths in your personal statement rather than writing an addendum that simply says, "I wish I hadn't partied so hard in college…"

Nontraditional applicants have an easier time overcoming this issue. Did you return to school later (for more college or for a graduate degree) and succeed? Serve in the military? Are you successful in a profession? Have more than five years passed since you graduated from college? Are you now a parent? Demonstrate that you bring an understanding of how the real world works, that you are an adult now, and that you understand what it takes to succeed in the things that really matter. Demonstrate that you know how to prioritize your life and that you make good decisions. Do not do this by using these phrases—do it by establishing credibility through the facts.

What If I Was on Academic Probation?

This is not discretionary—you must tell the schools if you've been on academic probation. For most schools, this means you had a GPA at or under 2.0. This needed information can be coupled with another GPA-related issue in one addendum.

What If I Took Time Off from School?

Schools ask on their applications whether you took any time off during your educational career. Describe whether you withdrew, took a leave of absence, or just decided not to attend. Explain your reasoning. You need to include dates and the reason for the gap in time. This is often combined with an academic probation explanation and/or a lack of maturity explanation.

How Do I Explain a Learning Disability?

If you are entitled to accommodations for a disability, you should absolutely request them through LSAC. There will be no markings on your application that you took the test under different conditions, so there is no downside to requesting accommodations.

Every year, I hear from a lot of people who have documented learning disabilities but are refused accommodations on the LSAT. I won't waste your time by going on a tangent about the evils of LSAC or why they refuse accommodations to so many people who have always received them or anything about the constant flurry of lawsuits thrown at them after people are refused accommodations. It might be because your reports aren't from the right type of professionals or because you perform in accordance with average test takers when you take tests without accommodations or because you refused accommodations in other situations. Many applicants are either refused accommodations or offered less than what they requested. I will simply say that if this happened to you, you are in very, very good company.

So what can you do about it in terms of explaining it to law schools? Draft an addendum where you state the facts, including:

1. date of diagnoses (including if it was reaffirmed after the initial test date);
2. type of disability diagnosed;

3. accommodations requested and received and performance as a result, particularly if you can compare it favorably to previous academic performance;
4. denial of requested accommodations on the LSAT, and why this is a problem for you given the exact nature of your disability; and
5. emphasis on the fact that your grades are a better indicator of your abilities to succeed because you were given necessary accommodations. Or, an explanation of why the academic nature of your work, in which you excelled, didn't require these accommodations.

Marni Lennon, assistant dean at the University of Miami School of Law, has more than twenty years' experience evaluating law school applicants and supporting students with disabilities. She says "there is a delicate balance between focusing on challenges and barriers and making excuses for less than stellar scores or your GPA. Identifying the ways in which you have worked hard to overcome challenges is an appropriate way to demonstrate your strengths and capacity to succeed in law school. If you are an individual who has a disability and are considering whether or not to share, you may wish to ask yourself the following: (1) To what extent does disclosure help the admission committee understand more about you and your determination, perseverance, and personality traits? And (2) How has your underlying disability fueled your commitment to study law, if at all?"

Many applicants "over-disclose." There is such a thing as *too much* detail about an illness. If you share too many facts centered on the people and systems that have failed you, and not about how hard you worked to succeed despite these circumstances, it can reflect poorly on you. If the information is conveyed with a negative or entitled tone, the reader will have concerns about your judgment and maturity and your ability to succeed in law school.

Sample Addendum 1

During my first ten years in the military, I put education on the back burner. I did finish high school, a promise I made to my mother, but college really wasn't on my radar. I was focused on getting promoted so that I could help my family. Additionally, I was volunteering for the most challenging assignments, in places that had limited education opportunities; there was no such thing as online education back then! After my last sibling left home and my mother could finally support herself, I turned my attention to my goals, which included pursuing a college degree. The year was 2004. At that time, I was a drill sergeant in navy boot camp, working sixteen hours a day, seven days a week. Going to a traditional university was not an option, and accredited online degree programs were very limited. I decided to enroll at the University of Phoenix.

Despite working long hours, I completed my associate's degree in 2006. Shortly after that, I was ordered to various deployable units and temporarily put my educational goals on hold. I served in four combat deployments over the next five years. One of those deployments was a tour in Al Asad, Iraq. My duties included supervising the Education Services Office. I was amazed that young marines were taking classes in between firefights with Al Qaeda insurgents. I decided I had no excuse and enrolled in a bachelor of science program. I specifically remember trying to finish a paper in a bunker one night during an attack. Imagine trying to focus on APA format with sirens constantly blaring warnings of incoming mortar fire! After I returned from Iraq, I was sent on two more combat deployments over the next two years. Despite having to juggle schoolwork with my duties as the command master chief of a fighter squadron actively engaged in combat operations in Afghanistan, I graduated *summa cum laude* from DeVry University.

Some may look at undergraduate degrees from the University of Phoenix and DeVry University and turn up their noses, but I know the challenges that I, and many other service members, had to endure to earn those pieces of paper.

Sample Addendum 2

I graduated high school in 1998 with the intention of attending college. However, since my family didn't have the financial means to pay for my education, I joined the Army National Guard to take advantage of the educational benefits.

When I finished training, I began working at a restaurant and focused my efforts on becoming a better musician and artist. By the time my obligation to the army ended in 2001, I found myself playing in an up-and-coming band, which meant I was constantly recording and touring. For the next three years, I immersed myself as a musician and promoter in the punk and indie rock scene in New York and New Jersey.

In 2003, I felt the urge to challenge myself in an academic environment, and I began taking classes at Union County College. It was during this period in my life that I also found myself becoming more interested in food and wine. Not soon after, I began managing the famous West Village cheese shop, Murray's. Managing Murray's and doing consulting work at restaurants began to interfere with my academics, and I put college on hold.

I would not attend college for another eight years, but after I returned to school in 2012, I never looked back. I continued to work in a bar/ restaurant full-time while attending college full-time until I obtained my bachelor's degree in 2015.

Sample Addendum 3

In 2006, I transferred to the University of California, Berkeley, from the City College of San Francisco. I soon found that my chosen field of study, mathematics, was too difficult given my participation in the school's tae kwon do competition team. I was too stubborn and proud to admit to myself that I was simply not as good at math as I had thought, and I spent three hours a day on the tae kwon do mat instead of studying.

Things got so bad that I was put on academic probation and subsequently dismissed from the university in 2008 because I was unable to bring my grades back up. I was told by the dean of students that if I could show that I could concentrate on academics the following semester at a community college, I would be given the opportunity to apply for readmission. The dean also advised that I should change my major. I did both. The semester following my dismissal, I took three classes at community colleges in two different cities and changed my major to English. I applied for and earned readmission back to Berkeley the following semester. I also quit the tae kwon do team.

Unfortunately, my mother was diagnosed with cancer right around the time I was readmitted to Berkeley. While I made significant gains academically, I was still coming up short in some classes due to my frequent trips back to San Francisco to care for my mother, who was by then undergoing chemotherapy. My father was unable to take time off during my mother's treatment, and my sister was living in another state, so it fell to me to care for her each day. This involved taking her to the doctor and her chemotherapy treatments, grocery shopping, and cooking lunch and dinner. I skipped classes frequently but made concerted efforts to keep up with the assignments as I was determined not to repeat my recent history of academic shortcomings. This kept up for about a year, until near the middle of my final semester.

After a long and winding road, I finally graduated from Berkeley in 2009. In the past six years, I have gained the maturity and focus necessary to succeed in law school without being derailed, as is also evident from my professional abilities.

What if I have to check "YES" on a Character and Fitness Question?
Have you ever been charged with a crime?

The most common affirmative responses to this question are due to driving under the influence (DUI), use of a fake ID, minor-in-possession citations, and shoplifting. Will these types of issues keep you from being admitted to law school? Potentially. The keys to a persuasive explanation are RECENCY and SEVERITY. Is it a one-time incident, or is there a pattern that might show substance-abuse problems and/or lack of judgment? This is where recency comes into play; if you've had a DUI and a possession arrest within the last year, it's going to be hard to show that you've had time to take your life seriously and turn things around. However, if you have one issue on your record from when you were eighteen, and you've kept your nose clean since, then it probably won't continue to plague you. That being said, you still have to report it.

You are being tested on candor—the worst thing you can do is lie on your application, get caught in the lie after spending $100,000 or more on your law degree, and not be able to practice law because you were found to be untruthful on your law school or bar application (when trying to get licensed to practice law). Better to own up to it.

Sample Addendum 4

On June 12, 2009, when I was twenty years old, a police officer spotted me while I vomited in a park. He approached me, stated that he smelled alcohol, and asked for my identification. Demonstrating further poor judgment, I handed the officer my friend's identification card. He asked me if this was really mine; I immediately owned to the fact that it was not, and I apologized. I was fully cooperative with the officer and was charged with underage drinking and possession of a fake ID. I went to court on August 14, 2009, and because the officer did not appear, the charges were dismissed. This incident served as a wake-up call for me: I now use better judgment with alcohol and have spoken to my fraternity about the dangers of underage drinking. In the four years since this incident, I have not violated any other laws and am in the process of having the charges expunged. I will update my application when this has occurred.

What If I Had an Honor Code Violation?

For obvious reasons, law schools hold law students and lawyers to a high standard of ethical conduct. You will have to take a course and a separate exam about professional ethics in order to practice law. You will then have a continuing obligation to take professional credits in the subject once you are a practicing attorney. So, if you have anything in your background where your ethics have been called into question, you need to be sitting up straight when you approach the moral character and fitness questions.

The most common violation that has to be reported is academic dishonesty. This includes plagiarism, cheating accusations, or anything along these lines that usually results in a student conduct/honor council proceeding and/or action or a failing grade as punishment for an academic conduct issue.

This is occasionally something that comes into play with international students when they first come to study in the United States because they are not necessarily aware that they need to cite to source materials or how to do it. If this is the case, and you made an honest (cultural) mistake and never had any incidents after the one where you learned this lesson, you will need to explain it. However, it may not detract significantly from your applications. I had a client in this situation who went on to earn very high grades after an occurrence of this sort, and, although his LSAT score was in the low 150s, he was admitted to several top fifty, and even a top twenty-five, law schools.

Even if your ethical incident did not fall into this category, my advice is to be honest about it, show that you have taken it seriously, and that it served as a learning experience/turning point for you. Remember to include dates, exact charges, and the process, etc. It's very important that you don't sound bitter, like you are blaming the professor or administration. Taking responsibility is essential to retaining your credibility. Otherwise, you risk sounding like a complaining problem child. As one law school associate dean said to me, "The other applications which drive me crazy are when they disclose an infraction but use most of the 'ink' to explain why it wasn't their fault. It wasn't my drugs. It was my apartment, but I wasn't drinking that night…It just doesn't ring credible and doesn't show the level of maturity that…I understand that any violation of the law in my car is my responsibility ultimately, and I learned…"

I also suggest that you obtain paperwork and/or a letter from the dean of students, who oversaw the conduct charge/incident to add credibility to your claim that you have since turned yourself around, that you completed everything that was asked of you, and that you are graduating in good standing. A statement of this type is sometimes referred to as a Dean's Certification or Dean's Letter.

What If I Have a Disciplinary Incident?

Did you smoke pot in the dorms? Throw a party that was too loud? Toss donuts off the balcony as part of a fraternity stunt? Yeah, I've heard it all before. You're entitled to a youthful indiscretion or two, really. I know there are some readers who won't take this advice, but the best thing you can do is report these incidents honestly. Don't overblow them (my girlfriend put the drink in my hand right before the cops came, and I am so terribly sorry, and I've gone to church every Sunday ever since, and I only drink one beer at parties now...)—just report them candidly, include the relevant details (and only the relevant details), and get out.

Sample Addendum 5

In May of my sophomore year of college, after final exams were complete, three friends and I decided to climb to the roof of our dorm and flash the onlookers as part of our year-end celebration. Unfortunately, one of the witnesses was the dean of engineering, who immediately called the head of residence halls. As we came out of the stairwell, the dorm supervisor pulled us aside and wrote us up for inappropriate conduct. We had to clean trash out of dorm rooms that had already been abandoned for the semester as our punishment. After we did this, our written disciplinary record was torn up. This incident is incredibly embarrassing and not at all indicative of how I have conducted myself in the last three years.

Do I Really Have to Report Speeding Tickets?

Most law schools exclude traffic violations from things that have to be reported under the Character and Fitness section of the application, but a few specifically include them. Please do not panic. If you can't remember the date or exact fine of the speeding ticket you got ten years ago, just approximate—provide the information to the best of your knowledge. If you recall the tickets, include the date, exact name of the citation, any pertinent details, that you paid the fine, that it was removed from your record, etc. This is pretty basic stuff, and unless you led police on a high-speed chase, this isn't the kind of thing that will have a negative impact on your application.

LSAT Explanations

The LSAT is the only objective piece of your law school application. It is the only way you will be judged exactly the same as everyone else; it's hard to be subjective about the results of a test that everyone takes under the same conditions. However, there are some circumstances when subjective value can be added, and it can work in your favor if you do it well.

Do I Have to Explain Multiple LSAT Scores?

When do you need to explain multiple LSAT scores, and when can you leave it alone?

Leave it alone IF:

- you took it twice and the scores are within three points of each other, and
- you simply have one cancellation and one score that you are sticking with.

Explain it IF:

- you think your pattern looks weird, like taking the LSAT three times and getting the exact same (or close) score every time— explain why you kept trying. What did you expect to be different the second or third time?
- you had a significant score increase. Why? Additional preparation? A bad test day? Being sick the day you took the test the first time? Distractions in the test center? A specific reason helps. Here are some examples:

Sample Addendum 6

When I took the LSAT in October 2015 and received a 152, I realized I had not put in the effort required to perform to my abilities on the test. This served as a wake-up call for me, and I set aside additional time for preparation. I decided to take a year off after college so that I could concentrate on the law school application process more fully. My September 2016 LSAT score of 164 is the result of my additional preparation and reprioritizing and is therefore a better indicator of my abilities.

Sample Addendum 7

My first LSAT score (166 in December 2012) was three points lower than my average score on timed practice exams. Therefore, I decided to retake the LSAT in February 2013. However, I got the flu three days before the exam and was still recovering when I took the test. I still felt weak. In hindsight, I exercised bad judgment by not canceling my score. When I saw my score (162), I felt that I had to redeem myself. Therefore, I took the June 2013 LSAT. Before the test, I was scoring in the 167–171 range on timed practice tests. Unfortunately, I received a 165 on the test. However, my persistence in continuing to try to reach my goals is evidence of my desire to excel.

Sample Addendum 8

Although I was consistently scoring in the mid-150s on timed practice exams, I received a 148 on the October 2013 LSAT. Unfortunately, I was seated by the front desk and found myself very distracted by talking and foot traffic. My December 2013 score (154) was not inhibited by these distractions and is a better representation of my abilities.

What if I'm Not a Good Standardized Test Taker?

If you have never taken a standardized test (e.g., if you attended community college and then transferred to a four-year university) or (for nontraditional applicants) it has been a really long time since you took a standardized exam, then this is something that should be pointed out in an addendum.

Likewise, if you were working full-time and/or devoted to family responsibilities while studying for the LSAT, you should share that information in an addendum. It helps to give the reader context for your score of which he or she might not otherwise be aware.

If you have a history of underperformance on standardized tests, you should explain this. The issue is, when do you have a history of under-performance and when do you simply *wish* you had done better on the test? If you have a score on the LSAT that is comparable to your SAT or ACT score in terms of percentile, and that score was low for your entering class in college, yet you performed superbly in comparison to your peers, then this helps prove your narrative that standardized tests don't reflect your abilities.

This argument does not work, however, if your grades in college were mediocre. It just isn't as compelling to say, "Although my SAT score was below the 50th percentile for my entering class at Cornell, my grades placed me in the top 50th percentile of my class." It is, however, compelling to say, "Although my SAT score was in the bottom 10 percent of my freshman class at Cornell, I earned a 3.89 GPA there, placing me in the top 5 percent of my class. Therefore, the SAT failed to predict my academic performance. Likewise, my LSAT score of 162 is not a good indicator of how I will perform at a law school where the 25th percentile LSAT score is 167."

If you simply really wanted to go to a top ten school (despite your 3.3 at a good but not amazing university and a 161 LSAT), then consider whether an addendum is really appropriate. If your LSAT score is consistent with your SAT score, and your SAT score was midrange for your college and your grades are midrange at your college, it's very hard to make the argument that standardized tests fail to predict your academic performance.

If you come from an underprivileged background, and you lacked the necessary support and resources to compete on standardized exams, this is absolutely worth sharing. This might include attending under-resourced schools, not having support at home, not being able to afford a prep course or tutoring, etc.

If your SAT score was high, but your LSAT score is low (because you didn't have time to prepare for the LSAT, or if you didn't get accommodations on the LSAT but you did on the SAT), this is another kind of argument you can make to show that the LSAT score isn't representative of your abilities.

Key Takeaways

- Things you may choose to explain in your applications include circumstances surrounding your LSAT and GPA.
- Things you must explain in your applications include interruptions in college attendance, academic probation, academic discipline or dishonesty issues, criminal charges, or related incidents.
- Stick to the facts; avoid bringing emotion into it.

CHAPTER 8

Building Your Résumé

I view the résumé as the greatest opportunity to share with a law school how you have spent your time. I believe this is the most underrated and overlooked aspect of the application process. Although applications may have you fill in basic information about jobs and activities, there is no room to explain things. If you do a great job on your résumé, by showing the law schools how you have spent your time and what you have accomplished, it frees up your personal statement to cover things that are more interesting and thoughtful about you. It's one thing to list a title of vice president of your fraternity. It takes it up a notch to explain that it was VP of Standards and Risk Management and that you had to handle the forced resignation of a fellow officer over some indiscretion, or that as Treasurer, you oversaw bringing the chapter out of debt and into a $10,000 surplus, and that you spent over hundred hours leading a committee to redraft the organization's bylaws. Likewise, instead of just saying you worked as a manicurist for three years, you can add that you worked twenty-five hours per week to fund your education. This is your chance to add the details of how you've spent your time.

The résumé, if properly executed, is what makes you a living, breathing, hard-working individual with interests and pursuits. This is your chance to not only show leadership but also share the extent to which you self-financed your education, describe your cultural or volunteer activities, language proficiencies, athletic talents, experience living in another country, how much you worked during college, and what your job as an office manager or sales associate or analyst or account executive really entailed and what you accomplished in each role.

Basic Rules of Résumé Writing

1. Avoid referring to yourself in the first person.
2. Use action words at the beginning of your descriptions.
3. Use past tense to describe things you did in the past and present tense to describe current duties.
4. It's okay to go onto a second page *if* you're doing it because of the substance and not because of the design you are using.
5. Do not include high school. Your high-school honors, athletics, and awards got you into college; now you need to stand on your accomplishments post high school. I know you might be thinking, "Well, that rule doesn't apply to me because I was high-school valedictorian/an Eagle Scout/captain of the football team and won an award for my community service." But to consider yourself special in this regard is a big mistake. Emphasizing high school often unwittingly highlights youth ("she was in high school three years ago?"), immaturity ("she thinks 'this' is important?"), lackluster college performance ("she didn't do so well once she moved out from under the watchful eye of Mommy and Daddy"), and privilege ("she went to *that* high school?"). Perhaps I sound cruel, but this is absolutely necessary to help you create an effective résumé.

Since you are an aspiring lawyer, you should know that every rule has an exception. Even I have made exceptions for those clients whose high-school accomplishments add context to their later achievements. For example:

- playing as a member of a professional symphony at age sixteen;
- participating in Olympic-level competitive figure skating;
- moving to the United States while in high school and learning English as a second language and still graduating from high school with honors;
- attending a fancy preparatory school on full scholarship when your socioeconomic circumstances would have otherwise prevented your attendance; and
- being an international student who attended boarding school in the United States or in another English-speaking country—you

may add this to your résumés to demonstrate experience studying in English.

How Should I Organize My Résumé?

Generally, the section headings for your résumé will include these main headers (if they apply to you):

- Education
- Professional Experience and/or Employment
- Activities
- Community Involvement
- Skills
- Accomplishments
- Interests

Be creative about the way you group different endeavors together. For example, I had a client this year with two separate passions and a lot of relevant experience in each—one was as a leader in the social action arm of a religious organization, and the other was as an advocate on issues relating to sexual assaults on campus. Rather than combining all of her experiences, we created separate headers ("Gender Advocacy" and "Jewish Community Service"). This way, her activities looked more focused, rather than sticking to a chronological listing, which would have made her interests appear scattered.

Education

Law schools are primarily concerned with your education, so lead with it. You should include all of your degree institutions and certificates, but you do not need to include every school you ever attended if you only attended for a summer, etc. You may include study abroad under this heading as well.

The Education section should include, in reverse chronological order, the schools you have attended since high-school graduation. Only in very rare circumstances should you include high school. One exam-ple of when it was acceptable to do so was for my client who was applying to the University of Texas, and she was trying to show ties to Texas that would not have otherwise been evident from other aspects of her back-ground (since she attended college in New York City).

Include the following information:

- Proper name of Degree, date conferred or anticipated
- Formal name of university, city, state
- Major/minor information
- GPA (if over 3.0)
- Honors (including graduation honors such as *magna cum laude*, thesis title, the number of semesters on Dean's List, honor soci-ety memberships, and scholarships and awards received, includ-ing descriptions if not self-explanatory)

Professional Experience

Include any jobs you've held since college, or before or during college if they were in line with an area of work you pursued, such as military experience, human resources, journalism, laboratory research, or teach-ing. If you have dabbled in a few fields, call this section "Professional Experience." But if you have one main area, you can give the section a specific title (e.g., "Laboratory Research Experience") and have a sepa-rate header for "Other Employment" (such as college jobs or summer jobs that do not fit into this category). Or, you can have one section for Teaching Experience and another for Real-Estate Experience if you've had more than one main career.

List every job you've held *since* high-school graduation. If it's been twenty years, you can leave some out, but for most applicants you will want to account for your time, even if it's not something that you think law schools will find impressive and even if it doesn't seem to be law related. You can choose to separate out post- and during-college employment through the use of headers, for example: "Experience" and "College Employment" or any variation that you feel fits your experiences.

This really should include all jobs because:

1. you are trying to account for your time;
2. there's no shame in showing a law school you're not above a little grunt work;
3. these jobs add context to your grades and other achievements, even helping to explain why you had a hard time with grades during a semester when you had to work full-time;
4. it demonstrates time-management skills;
5. it shows you weren't a recluse and that you had to deal with other people in a stressful or fast-paced environment; and
6. unglamorous or "menial" jobs build character and demonstrate a lack of elitism.

Exceptions to the "all jobs" rule are rare, but here are a couple:

1. If you made a living as a professional gambler, you might have second thoughts about sharing it. However, it can add character and an interesting aspect to your application. One of my clients who shared this story is graduating at the top of his class at Harvard Law School.
2. Jobs you held for a month probably shouldn't be listed by themselves. Instead, you could group together a number of temporary jobs and say something in the Personal section like, "Between March and August 2014, worked temporary jobs as an office administrator for various dental offices in the Detroit area."

When describing each job, try to include something specific. Instead of "sold and marketed homes" try "assisted in the sale of four homes, resulting in more than $3 million in sales." Avoid generalities ("learned valuable business skills") and especially those that sound like you're writing yourself an LOR. Avoid language referring to skills you learned, for example, "Learned to manage time and diverse coworkers in a fast-paced environment."

Avoid embellishing your experiences. Everyone knows what a legal assistant does, and it sounds disingenuous to write that you were drafting motions to dismiss and handling major trials singlehandedly. However, if you were promoted to senior paralegal and training other paralegals, you should share that. If you were promoted after only three months, include that too. If you took over the duties of the senior paralegal when he or she was out on family leave, that can be included. Just be careful about overstating your duties. It will set off alarm bells for admission officers and bring the credibility of the rest of your application materials into question.

Include the following information:

- Job title, name of employer, city, state (dates of employment).
- Include one to five bullets describing accomplishments and duties.
- Quantify success when applicable.
- Explain the purpose or focus of the organization/company if it's not going to be obvious to the reader.
- Start each bullet with an action word (e.g., coordinated, led, devised, arranged, planned).
- Avoid use of first person in the descriptions.
- Include the number of hours you worked per week or indicate full-time employment.
- As you're writing descriptions, consider whether the assessment would be better made by someone else (perhaps in an LOR) because it might sound arrogant for you to proclaim about yourself (e.g., "exercised brilliant decision-making skills").
- If you worked in a family business, own up to that because (1) it'll make more sense if it's not something in line with your interests and (2) it shows that you were probably handling a greater level of responsibility. Typically, in family businesses, so much is personally at stake, and one is naturally trusted with more oversight.

Activities

You should list each activity in reverse chronological order and include your role in the organization, the extent of your involvement, dates of involvement, and any particular accomplishments. This section should *include college and post-college* extracurricular activities and a description of the extent of your involvement in each. I believe that high-school activities should *not* be on a résumé for law school because the idea is that that's what got you into college, and you should have used your time in college to cultivate experiences for law school. However, if nothing on your résumé appears related to law, I see the argument for including your high-school mock-trial award *if* you won Best Delegate in the World. Just be judicious about including anything from high school; it makes you seem young and relatively unaccomplished, like you're reaching for a résumé filler.

Some tips about this section:

1. Don't refer to yourself as a "leader" unless you held a series of indisputable leadership positions. It can sound arrogant and misguided to say you are a "leader" because you were the scholarship chair of a service fraternity. Do not title this "leadership" unless you are using it to describe several organizations where you served as president. I've seen too many people call a section "leadership" and then list being philanthropy chair of their fraternity and a member of their high school's mock-trial team.

2. If you joined the prelaw society or Phi Alpha Delta your last year in school, it will look like an obvious résumé filler. State that you participated extensively, perhaps by saying: "Attended weekly events, helped coordinate law school panel events each semester, and actively worked with prelaw advisors and professors to create prelaw programming on campus."

3. Don't assume everyone knows what the "Blue Key Society" is, but do assume everyone knows what the "Golden Key Honour Society" is, and please spell it correctly because everyone knows how it should be spelled. You do not need to list the entire mission statement of Mortar Board, but should say that only twenty students of the senior class of eight thousand are selected for scholarship and leadership.

4. The point of sharing activities on your résumé is to demonstrate your interests and passions and to show that you seriously committed yourself to each. Therefore, stating your duties and accomplishments and the hours you spent devoted to the activity

will make your résumé more impactful. It's one thing to list, "Member, ABC," and it's another to list "Member, ABC (2015–17), actively involved in recruiting twelve new members in 2015 and twenty-two in 2016 as member of the recruiting committee, two hours per week." Much more impressive, right? If college was a while ago, and you either don't really remember or it would seem trivial in light of more recent accomplishments, you can simply list your activities like this: "Served as executive editor of student newspaper, president of International Students Association, and worked eight hours a week as a research assistant" by throwing it under the Education section in a single bullet.

Community Service

Do not include anything you did only for a day, like showing up for Relay for Life. If you've only done one or two community service events, and/or if your only community service activities have been through a Greek organization, do not have a separate section for these activities. This is an example of looking like you're exaggerating your experiences, and it lessens the credibility of other things on your résumé and in your application if law schools suspect exaggeration. This ends up highlighting a weakness (lack of time spent helping others) rather than making it a positive aspect of your application.

For nontraditional applicants, you can list professional organizations, religious organizations, sitting on nonprofit boards, canvassing for elections, and volunteering at your child's school. Dig deep for ideas; don't assume you have nothing worth including or that non-law-related things aren't of interest to schools. Many members of the military volunteer in communities where they are serving, and this is also worth including.

You can also use the résumé to show you're a well-rounded person. Here are some headers and potential things you could include underneath them:

Travel

Seeing the world is a good thing. Showing law schools you've seen the world is a good thing. When can it be a bad thing? When it sounds more like you come from a privileged family, and you tagged along with your parent to Turks and Caicos and Tahiti. A volunteer effort, especially for a prolonged period of time, is worth including. (If it was in high school, however, I usually take it off a résumé unless we are desperate for material). If you took the initiative to plan a cross-country road trip to visit Native American tribes, do share!

Interests

Include anything you consider significant, even if it demonstrates religious or political affiliation. These things add to diversity, and any law school that doesn't want you because of these affiliations isn't the right school for you anyway. Of course, if the group could be construed as a hate group or other group inappropriate for a future lawyer to be affiliated with, then I would leave it off the résumé. Good examples might include mountain biking or chess or a specific genre of fiction. You could also use this section to highlight athletic or musical talents, like if you were a Junior Olympic swimmer or an accomplished cellist. Consider these as potential interview or cocktail party talking points that make you memorable, likable, and/or relatable.

Accomplishments

These can include listing the marathons you've run and your finishing times, belt status for martial arts, Eagle Scout rank, published articles or poems, etc. If you have a series of publications, list them separately like you would in a CV, even if that means your résumé has a third page.

Skills

Think about your language fluencies, musical abilities, computer languages, etc. This section helps to show you are well rounded in ways that your transcripts, LORs, and other application materials may not reflect. Do not include computer skills such as "Social Media and Microsoft Office." These are now simply what I consider to be life skills and are not exceptional in any way. If you have been a legal secretary and are trying to show familiarity with billing and calendaring software, leave it off your résumé. It won't impress anyone, and it will be understood from your job description that you would be working with these tools.

Only include language skills if you would feel comfortable with an admission counselor calling you and speaking in that language. Also, don't include fluency in English; I should hope that's a given, even if—especially if—you're an international student. If you list another language, state how you obtained a level of fluency in that language. Was it spoken in your home? Did you live abroad? Did you study it in high school and college? For how many years? Have you passed a proficiency test in that language?

What NOT to Include on Your Résumé

You may have noticed three common résumé headings missing from my list: Summary of Qualifications, Objectives, and Relevant Coursework. Only include a Summary if you (1) have been working for more than five years in multiple positions or (2) are trying to pull together experiences that seem unrelated, and if you decide to incorporate this section, it should include concrete statements of fact rather than generalities such as "extensive history of providing excellent customer service." These statements are really only credible when someone else is saying them; on your résumé for law school, they feel like fluff.

Do not include an Objective section. Please. Your objective is to get into the law school you are applying to. That's it; don't state the obvious.

It's not necessary to list relevant courses because your transcripts are attached to your application. Besides, nearly all courses are "relevant" to law school since the law interacts with pretty much everything from engineering to international relations to art (copyright protection).

What Can I Add to My Résumé before Applying to Law School?

A lot of people ask me what they can do to improve their selection of jobs/activities to round out their résumés before applying to law school. If you still have at least six months before applying to law school, make an honest assessment of your experiences now that you've seen them on paper. Do your interests seem all over the map? Are all of your involvements surface level? Is there anything you can do this year to show growth in an existing interest, such as taking on a bigger role within a group or volunteer effort? Are you lacking real-world experience? Can you take on a part-time job? If you're afraid you don't look like a very serious person, can you become a research assistant or teaching assistant for a professor that would highlight a sincere academic interest and ability? If you've been working in one (non-law-related) profession for years, is there a volunteer activity you could undertake that would show a clearer affinity for studying and practicing law? Take time for introspection; it's seldom harmful to figure out your interests and gaps. Be proactive about adding depth or breadth to your experiences.

However, also keep this in mind: If you only have six to ten months before applying to law school, and you are also going to school and/or working, then the best use of your time is preparing for the LSAT. Don't sacrifice time on LSAT prep to build your résumé. Be sure you can balance both before taking on more at this point.

Sample Résumé 1 (Teaching Experience)
Education
The Johns Hopkins University, Baltimore, MD, Commencement: May 2013
Master of Science in Urban Education

- Cumulative GPA: 3.82/4.00.

Rhodes College, Memphis, TN, Commencement: December 2010
Bachelor of Arts in Political Science; Minor in Anthropology/Sociology

- Cumulative GPA: 3.37/4.00.
- Scholarships and grants totaling full tuition, room, and board.

Professional Experience

New Hope Academy, Baltimore, MD, November 2015–Present
Math Instructor; Special Educator

- Crafted individualized curricula for students with a range of cognitive and emotional disabilities.
- Differentiated and accommodated material in order to create rigorous, yet accessible, geometry and algebra II lesson plans for students with special needs.

The Village School, Houston, TX, October 2013—November 2015
Associate Teacher

- Responsible for implementing rigorous and engaging lesson plans for grade levels K–12 on short notice.

Baltimore City Public Schools, Baltimore, MD, August 2011–July 2013
ELA Instructor: Teach For America Corps Member

- Successfully managed middle- and high-school classrooms of more than twenty students with ages ranging from fourteen to twenty.
- Developed and executed English curricula for middle- and high-school over-/under-credited students in an accelerated credit recovery program at Baltimore Community High School (BCHS).
- Implemented data-tracking system and increased standardized testing scores by 28 percent from 2011 to 2012 at BCHS.
- Increased the cumulative reading level of ninth-grade students from 5.7 to 8.2 at Baltimore Talent Development HS.
- Served on the Instructional Leadership Team at BTDHS, as well as the Principal Search and Evaluation Task Force.

Philadelphia Public Schools, Philadelphia, PA, 2012
Summer School Social Studies Teacher

- Responsible for developing and implementing five-week summer school curriculum.
- Collaborated with a team of veteran and new teachers to determine strategies for increasing student achievement.

Sealy Independent School District, Sealy, TX, 2013
Summer School Substitute Teacher

- Remedial math lab instructor for Sealy Jr. High School.
- Instructed 6th and 7th graders in basic mathematical skills found on the Texas Assessment of Knowledge and Skills test.

Department of International Studies, **Rhodes College**, Memphis, TN, Spring 2013, *Research Assistant for Professor of International Studies (eight to ten hours per week)*

- Compiled reports concerning the human trafficking of women and children for the International Studies Department.
- Provided summary and analysis of activist advocacy efforts (both transnational and domestic) to combat trafficking.

National Civil Rights Museum, Memphis, TN, Fall 2012
Intern-Education Department (twenty hours per week)

- Created information packets and educational materials for schools attending the NCRM Freedom Awards and Gandhi-King International Peace Conference.
- Constructed, edited, and polished NCRM Comprehensive Civil Rights Timeline.
- Conducted interactive tours for museum patrons and school groups.

Activities
Court-Appointed Special Advocate, August 2016–Present

- Completed the certification and training necessary to serve as a court-appointed special advocate.
- Certified to represent the interests of abused and neglected children in the Juvenile Court system of Baltimore, MD, and present findings and recommendations to court in the form of a written report.

Pi Kappa Alpha Fraternity, 2006–2013
Philanthropy Chair (seven to twelve hours per week) 2007

- Organized the First Annual PKA Dodgeball Tournament, which raised over $1,000 for the local volunteer fire department.
- Created software program that tracks total community service hours performed by each member of the fraternity and introduced punitive sanctions for those not meeting the minimum requirements set by national headquarters. The combination of this program, along with the sanctions, increased the chapter's total philanthropy output from 640 hours in 2006 to 773 hours in 2007.
- Initiated the use of a designated driver hotline for seventy-six-member fraternity and organized the schedule of volunteers. This hotline is still in use by the fraternity and volunteering is now mandatory for all members.

Students for Barack Obama, Rhodes College Chapter, Fall 2008
Campus Coordinator (eight to thirty hours per week)

- Successfully chartered chapter and grew membership to include 122 students.
- Organized bipartisan voter registration drive between Rhodes College Democrats and Rhodes College Republicans, which registered 250+ students to vote in their respective states.

Rhodes College Admissions Office, 2007–8
Rhodes College Diplomat (three to five hours per week)

- Selected to direct interactive campus tours and promote the college to potential students and their families. Hosted prospective students during overnight visits (three to five hours per week).

Interests

- Avid marathoner: Completed at least one marathon or half-marathon in every city I have lived in the past five years (Memphis, Houston, Austin, and Baltimore).
- Competitive Olympic weight lifter.

Note from Ann: *This client's personal statement can be found in Chapter 9. This is a condensed version of his résumé where we emphasized teaching experience and duties so that his personal statement would be free to focus on his background and motivations for teaching. The dates of his positions have been changed in order to make the résumé more current for this book.*

Sample Résumé 2 (Traditional College Student)
Education

Emory University, College of Arts and Sciences, Fall 2015
Bachelor of Arts in Political Science, minor in Sociocultural Approaches to Media

University of Cape Town, South Africa, Spring 2014
Study Abroad

Relevant Experience

Modzi, Atlanta, GA   May 2015–Present
Vice President, Operations

- Serve as second-in-command at a start-up, nonprofit that operates in Zambia, providing mentorship and access to education for vulnerable youth.
- Work more than 40 hours a week and assist in managing five student volunteers
- Created the Bylaws, Articles of Incorporation, and Conflict of Interest Agreement.
- Drafted, submitted, and reviewed various grant and funding proposals.
- Created and standardized the organization's logo, tagline, and donor and student databases.
- Assisted in creating and maintaining the organization's promotional video, website, and social media pages.

Change-Magazine, Inc., Atlanta, GA   January 2015–Present
Public Relations Team Leader; Staff Writer

- Managed an intercollegiate team of students in charge of PR for 16 campuses nationwide.
- Worked over 20 hours a week, including running a weekly team meeting.
- Created, standardized, and distributed a variety of PR and marketing materials throughout the organization.
- Created an operational database of journalists and initiated a standardized journalist outreach program.
- Designed and edited a recruitment video now used on campuses throughout the country.
- Published two articles entitled "An Absence of Attention" and "Do as the Protestors Do."

Millennium Strategies, Atlanta, GA May 2014–August 2014
Research and Communications Intern

- Composed open letters and press releases, made press calls, and monitored press.
- Transcribed various interviews and speeches and organized and reviewed candidate reports and data.
- Expanded social media efforts and researched groups and individuals.

David Goodman Foundation, Atlanta, GA, August 2013–December 2013
#VoteEverywhere Ambassador

- Organized and administered Voter Registration, Get-Out-The-Vote, and Voter Education events.
- Marketed and publicized the Vote Everywhere Campaign and the Andrew Goodman Foundation.
- Attended weekly trainings and discussions about voter rights and youth engagement.

Congresswoman Nita Lowey, New York, NY May 2013–July 2013
Intern

- Answered office phones and drafted constituent letters.
- Attended and summarized congressional briefings and hearings daily.
- Assisted in scheduling staff and constituent meetings.

Activities
Emory College Council January 2015–Present
Junior, Senior Legislator

- Elected to represent the junior and now senior class on student government body.

- Responsible for various initiatives and legislation, including the expansion of Emory's composting program and the creation of a Webmaster position on College Council.

Oxford College Dance Team   May 2013–January 2014
Treasurer; Manager; Dancer

- Drafted and submitted budgets to the student government and organized and arranged practices, performances, and competitions.
- Attended practice six or more hours a week and ran stretches and warm-ups for 30 dancers.

Student Government Association (Oxford College at Emory University)
Secretary (May 2013–January 2014)

- Responsible for recording, publishing, and distributing meeting minutes and administering communications with students and faculty.

Freshman Senator (September 2012–May 2013)

- Served as representative of the freshman class and on the Transportation and Academics committees.

AmeriCorps Bonner Program   September 2012–May 2013
Bonner Leader, Bonner Service and Leadership

- Completed 312 community service hours at various locations, including an after-school tutoring and enrichment program for economically disadvantaged youth and a transitional housing program for single-mother families experiencing temporary homelessness; wages paid through government program.

Employment

Glocap Search, LLC, New York, NY   May 2015–Present
Temporary Administrative Staff

- Served as both a temporary administrative staff member and receptionist.
- Worked at various media, communications, and financial businesses.

Shorty's Pizza, Atlanta, GA   August 2014–January 2015
Server

- Helped train new servers on service expectations, restaurant protocols, and health and safety precautions; stopped working to recover from knee surgery.

Skills & Interests

- Conversational in Spanish.
- Classically trained in ballet, jazz, modern, hip-hop, and tap.
- Brand ambassador for theSkimm, a daily e-mail newsletter.
- International travel experience: Botswana, Canada, Dominican Republic, England, France, Greece, Israel, Italy, Mexico, Monaco, Portugal, South Africa, Spain, Turkey, Zambia, and Zimbabwe.

Note from Ann: *This applicant was admitted in her senior year of college to Columbia Law School under a Binding Early Decision agreement. Her GPA was under 3.5 and her LSAT was in the low 170s.*

Key Takeaways

- Include only activities *since* high-school graduation.
- Include hours per week for activities and jobs during the school year.
- Use facts to support your accomplishments.
- It's okay to have a two-page résumé (unless a law school tells you otherwise).

CHAPTER 9

Writing Your Personal Statement

What Is a Personal Statement?

This is the piece of your application over which you have—at present—the most control. And it's not to be taken lightly. A good personal statement adds to the application by tipping the scales in your favor. If someone with your numbers has a chance of being admitted to a particular law school, but not everyone with your numbers is admitted, the major deciding factor is the personal statement. A good LOR helps, but if you can't advocate for yourself, someone else advocating on your behalf isn't going to make your case for you. And, if the personal statement is unimpressive, the person evaluating your application may not even go on to read the LORs.

So, the personal statement is your chance to become more than a list of your accomplishments and experiences, more than your transcripts, and more than your LSAT score. This is your chance to be personable, likable, and impressive. This is your one chance to tell a law school what it wouldn't otherwise know about you. Don't blow it!

With that kind of pressure, it's understandable that this is the part of the application that makes applicants the most nervous. "I hate to write about myself!" you might be thinking to yourself. "I have no idea what to say!" you complain to your friends. "Nothing about me is unique!" you are screaming at your quasi-helpful parents or roommates. What do I say to those fears? Get over them. This is a great opportunity to consider what's most important to you, what motivates you, and what makes you *you*.

What Are Law Schools Looking for in a Personal Statement?

There are certain things a law school wants to be assured of: maturity despite youth, a commitment to the study of law, the ability to succeed in a rigorous environment, independent thinking skills, an understanding of the world around you, and feeling a duty greater than simple self-interest. Schools leave the topic pretty open to your choice. A good personal statement is interesting to read without needing to rely on shock value. It has a conversational rather than formal tone; it's not there to show how many big words you know, but rather to offer insight into your character. It lets a reader get to know you in a way they can't from other pieces of your application. And, hopefully, it also shows why a law degree is the next logical step for you.

Will I Use the Same Essay for Every School?

Pretty much. Some schools vary the length requirement, make a point of asking you to include why you want to go to law school and/or to their law school in particular, or ask you to focus on specific questions (e.g., at CUNY Queens). On my blog, you will find a list of all two hundred law schools and links to their personal statement requirements (http://lawschoolexpert.com/personal-statements/top-50-law-school-personal-statement-requirements/).

For most schools, however, the same personal statement will work. You will only tailor your essay to specific schools if (1) they ask you to do so or (2) you have a very specific reason for wanting to attend, and they do not ask for a "Why X Law School" optional essay.

How Long Should My Essay Be?

"Brevity is the soul of wit." So says Shakespeare, and so say deans of admission. Almost every time I help edit a client's essay from three pages to two, the essay is improved by trimming the fat. I have yet to meet an essay that couldn't be cut without sacrificing its power. Cutting the length requires you to really think about your message and decide what is essential to include. Some schools ask for only five hundred words, while others allow for up to four pages double spaced. However, most schools ask for a two-to-three-page (double-spaced) essay. Schools have length requirements for two reasons: (1) to test your ability to follow directions (keeping to the length requirement) and (2) to evaluate how well you write. For example, on the Columbia Law website, it states, "While there is no official page limit, a good guideline is two double-spaced pages, using readable fonts and margins. Your personal statement/essay should be clear, concise, and an example of your best writing" (http://web. law.columbia.edu/admissions/jd/apply/faq/application). This is pretty much the direction I follow when working on every essay—it should use every word wisely and tell an insightful story that shows why an admissions dean should enjoy (not just "appreciate" but actually "enjoy") having you at his or her law school.

How Do I Decide on a Topic?

Applicants struggle most with choosing a topic. It can be overwhelming. On any given day, I could choose to write about many different aspects of my life. For example, one day I might want to write about my experience as chair of a nonprofit board, or the next day about parenthood. The following week might have me wanting to reflect on starting my own business, or my experiences with the foster-care system. And, while I have a good twenty to twenty-five years of experience to choose from beyond what most law school applicants have, I think many applicants feel the same way. Do I write about my black belt in tae kwon do or being president of my sorority? Do I write about my internship with a Congress member or the year I spent recovering from an accident? How do I write about my leadership experience without sounding full of myself?

How do you choose a topic? I advise going negative before going positive. Make a list of your potential weaknesses as a law school applicant. I know, it sounds counterintuitive for an essay that is supposed to be a puff piece. However, taking an honest look at your weaknesses will help you decide what to show about yourself that is positive in order to counteract (indirectly!) any potential pitfalls. If you lack work experience and have never had to earn your own pocket money, you might appear to be a bit naïve or self-centered. Consider, then, sharing stories and experiences that put forth the opposite impression. Do you need to compensate for lackluster grades by demonstrating intellectual ability and maturity? As you're brainstorming topics, think about times you *have* shown these attributes.

Many applicants stress themselves out trying to figure out what makes them "unique." This is the wrong question to ask. There's so much pressure to be unique, to stand out. That's really not the point. Just think about who you are and what your best qualities and most meaningful experiences have been. Remove "uniqueness" from the equation and the pressure will be significantly relieved.

There is a misconception that personal statements must be about overcoming paralysis or poverty, or both. It's completely acceptable for someone who grew up with plenty of everything to want to attend law school and to deserve to get in. Just show some perspective and that you've done something meaningful with your life and that you've learned something relevant and insightful from your experiences (whatever they may have been). Some people say to me that "nothing really bad has happened in my life, so I have nothing to write about." And, conversely, some people say to me, "But isn't everyone a child of immigrants who came to this country with nothing who has to help their parents navigate the system?" I think everyone believes his or her own experiences are ubiquitous to some degree. Don't worry about others sharing the same story. After all, that just makes your experiences relatable to the reader. Write what is true for you.

The goal is to present a picture of yourself as someone who is ready for law school. You do not want to do this by directly addressing the question ("I'm ready for law school because..."), but rather by telling a story that shows that you are a thinking person, someone who has experienced life, understands how the world works, and who brings something to the table that adds to a law school's class. You can do this by sharing a story about how your family background taught you the importance of working hard for what you want or how running a student organization taught you to deal with different situations/people. You can write about how your first career taught you what is most important as you embark on your second career, or how a particular experience sparked your interest in law.

Law school decision makers are also concerned with whether applicants have given serious thought to their future careers so that you do not turn out to be an unmotivated and/or disgruntled graduate of their law school. You want to avoid sounding overly idealistic ("I want to be an international lawyer" from someone who speaks only English or "I want to create lasting change in the world" from someone who hasn't done more than a few philanthropic events through his fraternity). It's an important exercise, while brainstorming for your personal statement, to articulate why you want to attend law school. It's a good personal exploration to undertake and may help shape your personal statement. Some schools ask you specifically to address motivations for studying law in their personal statement prompts. For example, here is Boston College's:

"We are interested particularly in learning about your motivation and preparation for the study of law as well as any circumstances that you believe relevant to the evaluation of your credentials." (http://www.bc.edu/content/bc/schools/law/admission/applying. html#procedure.) While you don't have to address this for every law school you apply to, it is a good exercise to try to articulate it and to keep in mind that you will want to work it into some essays based on some schools' prompts. And, it will definitely be asked of you during any interviews you might have with law schools.

When Should Something Be Your Personal Statement Topic as Opposed to Your Diversity Statement and/or Addendum?

If you are choosing a topic to explain circumstances surrounding poor grades in college, consider saving this story for your addendum and using your personal statement to address something positive. I had a client who originally wrote about a serious injury that set him back during college, but we ended up using this story explain a year of poor grades in college in an addendum. This freed up his personal statement to address how a small-town country boy went on to get his masters in international policy overseas. Then he could write a diversity statement that piggy-backed on this by concentrating on the socioeconomic background of his family and the poor level of educational resources in the town where he was raised. So, between these three documents, the reader got a really thorough glimpse into how three different aspects of his background overlapped and added to his perspective and experiences.

One of my clients wrote her personal statement about how being the child of immigrants motivated her to succeed in school but developed a different angle of this story (focusing on reliance on the kindness of others and the sacrifices made by her parents) for her diversity statement.

"While ten students may write about their immigration experiences and hurdles overcome, the most compelling essays give insight, by way of specific examples, of what a day in the life of the applicant was like. They focus on pivotal moments, forks in the road, inspiring teachers, activities which gave them confidence and the ability to learn more about themselves and others, etc.," says Lennon.

How Do I Begin?

Don't skip directly to drafting your essay. If you do, you'll be eliminating a lot of potentially fabulous ideas. Your first idea is not necessarily the best and, if you get too invested in writing that draft without exploring other potential topics, you may get frustrated later when someone gives you feedback that isn't especially positive. I also think it's dangerous to read sample essays because no two stories are the same. Additionally, just because one person wrote it doesn't mean (1) it's good, (2) it's the reason he or she got into law school, or (3) that it is the same kind of story you should be telling or voice you should be using to write about your life experiences.

It's better to really explore different topics before deciding on a direction. Once you've decided on a direction, then start drafting.

How Do I Brainstorm Topics?

When brainstorming topics, I find it can be helpful to answer some thought-provoking questions. Review my suggested list below, sit down, and write as much as possible in response to a few of them over, let's say, thirty minutes. This will help you to figure out which subjects are easy to write about and which feel like a stretch. When doing this exercise, try answering the following questions:

- What would surprise law schools (or even your best friends) to learn about you?
- What experiences in your life lead you to law?
- What is your proudest accomplishment and why?
- What is the hardest thing you've ever done and what did you learn from it?
- Why did you choose a certain experience on your résumé, and how did it help you grow?
- How did your family life impact your decisions and experiences?
- What is a skill or attribute that defines you, and what facts/stories from your background demonstrate that?
- What motivates you?
- Who inspires you?
- In what ways have you grown and/or have your views changed during (or since) college?

Case Studies

The following are some examples of different applicant archetypes and how to present yourself given your backgrounds and perceived weaknesses. These approaches are not meant to be formulaic, but to serve as examples of what you should think about when deciding how to present yourself to law schools. These examples should help open your mind to new and creative approaches. It is certainly not intended that you should follow these examples to the letter as some sort of recipe for success. Rather, I share these in hopes that they serve as inspiration to people in similar situations.

Professional Actor/Dancer/Musician

Law school applicants with artistic backgrounds often worry that they won't be taken seriously in the process. However, I've seen actors, musicians, artists, and dancers get into great law schools when they emphasize certain aspects of their backgrounds. For example, one of my clients wrote a compelling personal statement about how he developed from each of his majors (one in theater and one in a pre-law subject). Another theater major wrote about how he learned to work hard and do grunt work in summer stock, and how this has translated to his other endeavors. A professional dancer wrote about how she developed an eye for detail that applies to her professional endeavors today. Recently, I worked with an actor who talked about how playing a role as a gay male made him more aware of LGBT equality issues and more understanding of current headlines. Each of these applicants were very successful at getting into reach law schools, even though they were initially worried that they would appear to be giving up on an artistic dream for a more pragmatic choice. You should also notice that none of them wrote about wanting to represent artists upon becoming an attorney; that statement can come across as both unrealistic and cliché. It is important to show how law school fits into your goals, but it doesn't have to be so predictable as picking an area of law to practice. If it does so naturally, fine, but you do not need to force it in order for your story to make sense.

Simply considering the viewpoints of others as an actor, for example, is relatable to law. Likewise, I've worked with musicians who have equated their love of jazz with a love of history and civil rights and a composer who talked about the analysis and thought required by his craft and how he wanted to put those skills to use helping others.

Teach for America

Want to influence public policy on education now that you've been in the classroom and seen the impact of education inequity? Neat. I believe you and I believe in what you are trying to do, I promise, but it's been said by every TFA participant who ever applied to law school. TFA is a great program, with great training, and they pick the best and brightest. It's a credibility-builder with law schools, and social justice is something law schools care about, so you are already ahead. But if you're going to write about this in your personal statement, try to take a different approach with it (like special education advocacy or a specific problem you encountered that a law degree would enable you to solve) or highlight something else about your background and leave TFA to an LOR and to your résumé.

One personal plea: if you are a TFA person, *please* don't tell me the story of poor little Micah or Isabelle, who comes from a family living in poverty and how he or she faces every disadvantage and how, by working with his or her family, you learned X and Y...This is not your story. When Micah or Isabelle applies to law school in fifteen years, I look forward to reading their essays about how a teacher inspired them to reach higher and help others. But their story is not your story, and your personal statement needs to tell something personal about you. It can't focus more on someone else just because you led a privileged life. Focus on choices you've made, things you've learned, and goals you've developed that have been inspired by your experiences. Make sure you have plenty of "I" statements. This is a good test to see if the essay focuses enough on your experiences and insights. If you have only one "I" statement per paragraph, the essay might not focus enough on you.

Study Abroad

Studying abroad is so common now that, for about eight or nine years, I've had a rule with my clients—no essays about studying abroad. For a while, it was cute to read stories about how the lights turned on automatically in the stairwells in Italy and how you learned to drive on the left in London or Melbourne, but now these things have lost their luster because they end up sounding naïve or banal. Now, I will sometimes have my clients discuss an abroad experience in the context of other things they've done. For example, if your passion is for global human rights and you participated in a study abroad program that included an internship with The Hague, then this would be an interesting thing to discuss in a personal statement. A good rule of thumb is that if it reads like a travel essay, it probably isn't a good personal statement topic. Later in this chapter, I include an exception to this rule from a client who studied in Paris in the aftermath of the terrorist attacks and her experiences during that time, simply to show that there are exceptions to every rule.

The Scattered Soul

Have you dabbled in a lot of things but not become the master of any? Emphasize that you take initiative in the things you do and that you learn from each opportunity. Demonstrate that you are not just a person skating through another boring summer–show that you really put effort into understanding the field. One of my clients maintained a crafts blog and another monitored an online gaming community; both are now graduates of top fourteen law schools. Don't underestimate what you have going for you—even if it feels unrelated to law school. Think about what you've done that shows intellectual curiosity, engagement in issues that you care about, dedication, and tenacity. Spin a lot of different interests into being curious about the world, wanting to make an impact in many ways and/or being open to learning new things and meeting new people.

Internships

If an internship is well described on your résumé, and especially if it is supported by an LOR, you do not also have to address it in your personal statement, even if you think it's the most impressive thing about you. Think about how things are balanced throughout your application. Many people write about internships because they feel they *should*. I recently spoke to a pre-law group at a large public university and asked, "Do you guys feel a lot of pressure to accumulate internships?" The entire room nodded emphatically. Internships, by themselves, are not necessarily worthy of great attention in your personal statement.

You should only choose to emphasize your internships in a personal statement if you learned something specific in a unique situation, were able to contribute meaningfully, or learned something significant while having a negative experience at an internship. Think about what makes the experience compelling. Simply having the internship on your résumé and explaining your duties may be enough to "get credit" for it, opening up your personal statement for something more insightful about your character and experiences. But, if you can show initiative, that you are self-motivated, that you give yourself the freedom to make mistakes and learn from them, and that you exercise good judgment and independent thought, this will go a long way toward presenting your internship experiences effectively in a personal statement.

One of my clients had a very strong GPA from a very good undergraduate school and an LSAT score just below the 25th percentile of most of the top ten schools. Her résumé was packed with everything pre-law, including a thesis on a constitutional issue. Her personal statement, rather than being a cheerleading piece for her résumé, was about learning that she was not meant for political work after spending a summer working on Capitol Hill. She graduated from Yale Law School.

This year, I had a client with significant internships in the Republican Party in a Southern state. She wrote a beautiful essay about how she was often the only female in the room and the ways in which she was treated differently and disrespected, and how she had to work more than twice as hard as the males surrounding her in order to get real responsibilities and promotions. This was a brilliant example of how to approach an essay that is—on its surface—an internship essay but is really an insightful take on work ethic and gender discrimination that remains pervasive.

Significant Experience in Real Estate, Finance, Entertainment, Computer Science, etc.

Many people are applying to law school after having already experienced one or two (or more) careers. If you worked on projects that interacted with law, this can help you provide a good tie-in to a natural switch to law school. Attributes such as problem solving and working as part of a team definitely transcend careers. If you were self-employed, you can repackage your experience as knowing how to run a business and how to serve clients. You can use your work experience to show problem-solving skills, people skills, and other experiences that will prove helpful as a lawyer in private practice. Demonstrate that you know what you are getting yourself into with the financial and time investment of returning to school. Law schools will appreciate your maturity and thoughtfulness about your next career steps.

Paralegal

Many recent college graduates spend a year or two in a law firm learning the trade, and this is really valuable preparation because it shows that you have a realistic understanding of the practice of law. Whether you intend to return to the same type of practice after graduating from law school or if this experience has soured you on a certain type of law or legal environment but your drive to practice law remains intact, law schools appreciate your time as a paralegal. This year, I had one client write about what it took to put a deal together and why she thrives on all-nighters—she got into Georgetown with a 160 LSAT. Another client wrote about how her job as a paralegal brought her to a foreign country for an extended trial and what it was like to be on the night shift far from home.

The possibilities are really endless. One thing you really have going for you is a clear understanding of what lawyers do and what it takes to be a successful attorney. You know the kind of attorney you want to be and the kind of attorney you pray you'll never become. Use this to your advantage! You could write about the longest day you had, the hardest thing you did on the job, the attorneys who are your mentors, and the ones who treated paralegals disrespectfully. What did this experience teach you about your future career (good and bad)? Was there a particular case that moved you or frustrated you? Present your experiences insightfully rather than simply repeating your job duties. Leave that to your résumé. And leave an evaluation of your skills to an LOR. Focus on what you learned and how you grew through your experiences as a paralegal.

What Should I Avoid?

Are there some topics that, as soon as someone runs them by me, make me cringe? Yes. Some should just be avoided. Generally, I urge people to stay away from an essay that revolves around high school. You can use childhood experiences to provide context for later decisions/events that you will be discussing, but they shouldn't be more than a third of your essay. If you suffered a traumatic event as a child that created the necessity for you to work full time while in school or remain close to home, there is a good reason to share that event because it provides context for your later achievements and decisions. High-school sports should never be mentioned. Ever. Neither should high-school mock-trial competitions. These are the things that got you into college. What have you done since then to get yourself into law school? What you did as a teenager while under a parent's roof is not going to impress anyone, unless you are the person who is applying to law school at age eighteen. A good rule of thumb: if it could've been your college admission essay, it shouldn't be your law school personal statement (It could, however, in some circumstances, be a diversity statement).

Here are additional examples of other topics to avoid:

- the injured athlete who struggled to find his or her way after no longer having the structure and support system of the team;
- study abroad, particularly of the "learning to drive on the other side of the road" variety (as discussed above);
- writing about an event that the entire country experienced as being your impetus for applying to law school, unless you were intimately involved or directly impacted (However, writing about how 9/11 changed your experience as a Muslim American could be an impactful diversity statement);
- sharing a story that really makes you a high-maintenance complainer, such as the time you fought the dean of your school over your B+ that should've been an A-, or that makes you sound like a victim (of things that weren't crimes or tragedies). However, if you challenged a school policy in a way that the school/administration respected, and they later brought you on board to work with them on that issue, then it's a fabulous essay topic;
- a childhood dream of becoming a lawyer, particularly one that includes a cute story about how you negotiated your bedtime or decided to become a lawyer after watching a certain TV legal drama;
- cute childhood stories generally; and
- anything that you use as cocktail-party conversation, like the time you were chased by a bear while hiking (unless you were attacked and airlifted out, like one of my former clients, in which case you

may find it more effective to put this in a diversity statement if you had to spend significant time recovering or in an addendum if your recovery impacted your GPA or created a gap on your résumé).

No matter what topic you choose, here are things to watch out for and eliminate from your personal statement:

- arrogance and elitism;
- a purported drive to serve others and to "be a voice for the voiceless," where this is not supported by anything you've actually done in the past (avoid trite statements);
- a focus on someone else's challenges and how they inspired you;
- résumé bullets (here's what I did and when I did it, and here's what I did next);
- a laundry list of everything you've ever done (boring!);
- lots of conclusions with few facts to back them up (a good personal statement never has to say, "I always wanted to be a lawyer," or "I overcame obstacles" or "I work hard" because the story being told convinces the reader to come to this conclusion on his or her own. Remember what your high-school English teacher taught you: show, don't tell.);
- a lack of specifics and a narrative that goes around issues instead of addressing them directly;
- spelling and punctuation errors;
- excessive use of passive voice;
- a story that is "too" memorable (some applicants believe the main goal is to be super memorable so that the reviewer gasps aloud, but this really only happens in two cases: (1) when an essay is so ridiculous that it becomes a joke in the admissions office or (2) when an applicant's life story is so compelling it demands absolute and complete authenticity.);
- treatises on the importance of law in society;
- quotes by famous people, not said directly (and only) to you;
- artsy/poetic efforts that are distracting;
- a failure to follow directions or answer the question being asked;

- a lack confidence in yourself (unfortunately, this is mostly a problem with women when they write about themselves. I don't think I've ever had a male client write something like, "I struggled with finding my voice in the group." Think about the gender biases we impose upon ourselves and fight them.);
- an inclusion of the school's name as a fill-in-the-blank without saying anything meaningful about the school; and
- the use of any of the following words or phrases:
  — **"Personally."** It's a personal statement. By you. Of course it's personal.
  — **"In Conclusion."** Blech. Just conclude. Don't announce that you're concluding.
  — **"I believe."** It really doesn't matter what you believe about your ability to succeed in law school. The fact that you believe it is immaterial. Just state the facts so that the reader independently concludes that he or she believes what you are trying to prove. (Same with **"I think"**).
  — **"Unique."** Very few things in this world are unique, especially the use of the word "unique."
  — **"Firsthand."** I think it goes without saying that your experiences are firsthand. What else would they be? And if they were secondhand, why would you write about them?

What Should My Introduction Look Like?

I want to learn one relevant fact about you from the first sentence of your essay. I do not care if you have a "hook" or a clever, attention-getting device. I would prefer something straightforward and professional that gets me interested in you right from the beginning. I do not want you to introduce your story with vague statements like "My life has been a journey" or "I am the culmination of my experiences." These are lame statements, not only because they can be heard on any episode of *The Bachelor*, but also because they apply to everybody. I learn nothing about you. Instead, start with a fact. Below are a few examples with some explanations of what the applicants were trying to accomplish. These examples demonstrate how an introduction sets the tone for the entire essay.

From each of these introductions, you can imagine how the essay will proceed—and that's the whole point.

Area of Specialization

"I sat in a lecture hall at New York University School of Law, completely surrounded by men with some—or less—hair. Timidly, I glanced at my fellow attendees. Would they accept me as a member? I tried to listen to the conversations happening around me, and find a time to join in, but it seemed like everyone had known each other for years. I had just joined the Copyright Society of America."

This client had a great LSAT score and poor grades, and her résumé was heavy on artistic endeavors. By writing about her involvement in the Copyright Society, she demonstrated a clear reason for attending law school and showed she had the chutzpah to take the initiative to accomplish her goals. She got into Fordham Law School off the waiting list and is now a law graduate and general counsel for a corporation in New York.

Young Applicant

"I spent only three short years in college, but I used them to the fullest, often taking sixteen to twenty credits a semester to explore subjects not required for my major. My education was enhanced because, once I began a subject, I continued to explore it in as many ways as I could."

This client only had two years of transcripts by the time she submitted her application. We wanted to show that there was more to her transcripts than met the eye. Yes, her grades were very good, and she had internships with a large corporation, but she was also more than just those things. Her essay went on to describe her interest in religion, the environment, math, science and law, and how her interdisciplinary studies helped her grow and gave her direction for her career. She was admitted to several top fourteen schools.

International Student

"I came to America by myself when I was seventeen. I wanted to attend college in the United States, but without knowing a word of English, it seemed like a

distant dream. I chose to attend a boarding school in order to immerse myself in an English-speaking environment. My dedication to academic success in a new language took many forms, including studying in the restroom every night, after lights-out in the dorm."

This essay focused on dedication by showing how the writer was willing to put in long hours to reach his goals. It described how he taught music lessons during college (mostly in exchange for free food) and that even as he transitioned out of music as a professional, he kept the same dedication and applied it to all of his other endeavors.

Overcoming Addiction Story

"I have been a recovering alcoholic since June 14, 2007. While addiction is a lifelong struggle, with the support of family, friends, and my intense desire to make something of my life, I have demonstrated—through my commitment to education and to service—that I am prepared for the demands of the legal profession."

This client took a leave of absence from college to participate in rehabilitation and then returned to a nontraditional college program. He excelled and was granted acceptance to the regular degree program, where he continued to excel. His essay talked about this and how he went on to mentor troubled youth. With a very high GPA and a low-150s LSAT score, he was admitted to several reach schools. He chose to attend a top one hundred school, where he was in the top 5 percent of his class. He then transferred to, and graduated from, Georgetown Law.

Previous Career Unrelated to Law

"A computer programmer, a physicist, an immigrant from Vietnam who never graduated from high school, a taxi driver, and a young man wearing a backward baseball cap are all sitting around a table with me. We are chatting and laughing. In most circumstances, we appear to be an unlikely group. However, the wide variety of people I meet and interact with is one of the things about poker that I find most interesting."

This client had an undergraduate degree from Berkeley with unimpressive grades and more than a few years of floundering before deciding to apply to law school. Her personal statement showed thoughtfulness and sophistication, shared a very different side of poker with the reader, while shattering stereotypes: she explained how poker players banded together to raise money for someone among their ranks who became ill. She is now a graduate of the University of California at Irvine College of Law.

Family Experience

"My parents did not want us to associate work with monetary gain alone, but rather with life itself. For me, hard work is as regular as waking up in the morning and, when you grow up on a ranch with five siblings, that means getting up at 5:00 a.m.; any later and you risk an additional two hours of shoveling horse manure."

This client went on to discuss how her family was able to adapt when the recession hit and how working hard—and with a positive attitude—paid off when she worked selling cars and when she faced a serious health issue. This client had a low-140s LSAT score and a 3.5 GPA. Her essay about hard work led to her admission to several law schools where the median LSAT score is fifteen points higher than hers.

Parents as Attorneys

"Despite their common profession as attorneys, my protective Chinese mother and jolly, comforting Caucasian father raised me from very different perspectives."

This client had a 3.9 and a mid-160s LSAT score. His essay went on to talk about how different his parents' careers were and how each one influenced his desire to be a lawyer. He is a graduate of the University of Pennsylvania School of Law.

Student Leadership

"You're doing your job all wrong, man. The point of this team is to travel and drink, especially as the man in charge."

This client went on to write an essay about how he took initiative and changed the culture of an organization for the better. Instead of talking about his research, writing, and argumentation skills developed through Model UN, he focused on leadership. His essay is included in the samples later in this chapter.

"Being thrown into the fire of my fraternity's executive board as a freshman helped me develop as a leader."

This client spent a lot of time as a leader of his fraternity, so we used examples from his leadership experiences that showed the business and people skills he developed as treasurer and then president of his fraternity and how he worked to bring the organization to a better place. The idea was to make his skills transferrable to the real world to make up for the fact that he lacked work experience.

Diversity Topic as Personal Statement

"Bombay Riots, India, 1992: It was all very real to me. The Hindu Muslim riots that shook the country, and the world, were happening on the streets outside my house. I have a vivid memory of seeing my father bring his guns out, layer our terrace with broken glass, and keep watch throughout the night. This is my first memory associated with religion."

Her essay then went on to say how she opened her mind to all religions and even served as president of the Jewish Students Association in college. Her diversity statement dealt with her experiences growing up in India more specifically.

Second Career/Postgrad Work Experience

"Years ago, I thought that I would have to wait until I became a successful professional to do anything meaningful with my life. When my original career plans in veterinary medicine unexpectedly changed, however, I realized I could make a difference by simply using the resources I already have at my disposal."

This applicant was in her forties. She had to leave graduate school more than twenty years prior because of family responsibilities. In her essay, she wrote about how she strove to help others' lives as much as she could without a law degree, but that this was finally the time to pursue law as a means of serving others.

"Before fully committing to a law degree, I pursued a career in tech. This proved worthwhile not only because it taught me invaluable problem-solving and interpersonal skills but also because the perspective I gained confirmed and reignited my passion to practice law, while also narrowing the fields of law I'd like to practice."

This applicant had a few years of experience working in marketing and worried that it wouldn't translate well to law school, so this was a great way to address that perceived negative head-on. She went on to write about exactly what her introduction explains, giving concrete examples, and even addressing what she learned as a woman in a male-dominated industry and how that experience will help her in the legal profession.

How Do I Conclude My Personal Statement?

People try to make their conclusions mirror their introductions by referring to something cute or clever, bringing the essay full circle. I don't think this is helpful or necessary. Personal statements do conclude somewhat formulaically. It's a short essay—you bring the story forward and end with where you are today; there's no reason to refer back to the beginning of your story, as it should've grown and progressed naturally. Lawyers make their arguments, conclude clearly (not cleverly), and get out. Your personal statement should do the same. The body should make your case, and the end doesn't need to repeat, echo an opening remark, or bring anything back around to the beginning. Especially if it risks being cheesy. Rather, your essay should end with something about law school, pretty much every time, and pretty much without exception. How did the experience you shared lead you to law school? How did it help you develop qualities that prepared you for law school? How did it help you develop interests that you hope to explore in law school and/or at a particular law school? Addressing one or more of these issues (depending on your personal statement topic) is the way to conclude an effective and persuasive personal statement.

Likewise, avoid naming the school in your conclusion. Adding a fill-in-the-blank conclusion with a school's name is a common mistake. First, it's pretty meaningless to just throw that in at the end without adding substance, and if you add something about why you want to go there it has to fit with your personal statement to avoid sounding clunky or tacked on (So don't do this unless a school asks for it in its prompt, such as with the University of Maryland). The big mistake happens when you send the wrong personal statement to a school. Lawyers handle details.

That's what they do. Don't mess this up. Michigan doesn't want to know how much you want to attend Duke; in fact, they might just take you up on it.

How Do I Format My Essay?

The standard rule is to use a serif-font (with little lines on the end of letters), in twelve-point font, double-spaced, with one-inch margins all around. Use a header that has your name, LSAC ID#, the title "Personal Statement," and page number on each page of every document you upload with an application. Do not use a creative title. Ever. I see people try things like "A Journey to Law" or even something they perceive as clever, and it never works. It feels unprofessional.

Format all of your application materials similarly—make sure fonts and headers are consistent so that things look streamlined rather than piecemeal.

> TIP: After every draft, (1) set it aside for a day and (2) read the draft out loud before making further edits. This helps to catch grammar errors and to smooth out awkward transitions. You can also record yourself and listen to it afterward to notice additional details and how your story flows. It helps you catch repetitive language too. Finally, read the piece backward—yes, backward. You'll notice all those errors that your eyes and brain automatically correct based on what they expect to see.

Personal Statement Examples

I do not believe in reading or relying upon personal statement samples, but I am defying my own rule by including some in this edition of the book. I believe sample essays are problematic because they encourage you to follow another's example rather than crafting a tone and story authentic for you. They can also make you feel badly because you worry your experiences don't measure up to the samples. However, I decided to include a variety of personal statements that my clients have used successfully in this book because I want you to see that you don't have to write the most memorable essay that has ever been written and that it's not about being clever or creative. I also want to show you the variety of people who go to law school so that you can see there is not just one clear path. Please note, these essays have been sent to law schools, and plagiarizing any part of them would be immediate grounds for disqualification of an application.

Diversity as Personal Statement Topic

I am from the Bayview-Hunters Point district of San Francisco. Unless you are from the Bay Area, you have probably never heard of it. Most people think of the Bay Area as a binary world of excesses, with the opulence of San Francisco on one side of the bay and the crime of Oakland on the other. That characterization is far from accurate. The Bayview is where the poorest of San Francisco's marginalized live. It is where all the major gangs hold court and where a vast majority of the violent crime in the Bay Area occurs. It is a ghetto not dissimilar from most others in that if you are from there, you are more likely to become a statistic than to make it out alive. I count myself as being very fortunate for beating the odds.

I grew up surrounded by violence. My earliest memory is that of my next-door neighbor shooting his son in the back because he stole drugs—this happened in front of my house. The house on the other side of me was a crack house. Across the street lived the head of a local gang. I heard gunshots from my bedroom window every night. Just walking out my front door was reason enough to fear for my life. Obviously, if we could have lived anywhere else, we would have. My family was not always on government assistance, but I am not unfamiliar with the pain of going hungry and the embarrassment of asking for help. My house had rats in the walls, holes in the ceiling, and mold in the garage. Pollution and contamination from a local power plant was shown to have caused an abnormally high amount of health concerns in the Bayview, and that holds true for my neighbors and my family: from the hives I still get upon the slightest disturbance to my skin, to my mother's uterine cancer.

Even given all of that, I still count myself as having been very fortunate. I have two loving parents, which far exceeds what many from my neighborhood can claim. My mother grew up as the daughter of a working-class family in Hawaii, moved to the mainland as soon as she turned eighteen, and worked as an office assistant until I was born. My father was a young black man in Los Angeles during the 1960s and was in and out of prison until he decided to turn his life around by attending San Francisco State University in his thirties. After my father graduated from college, he quickly realized the great value of education. He had struggled for a long time with finding stable employment, partly because of the cyclical nature of this country's criminal justice system and because he lacked the necessary credentials to even get in the door. My parents were determined to give me the tools to get myself out of the ghetto by investing in my education.

My neighborhood elementary, middle, and high schools to which I was automatically assigned, but thankfully did not attend, were and are terrible. By way of example, the high school that I could have gone to is infamous for having graduated only 10 percent of its black seniors in 2009. When I think of my educational career thus far, I often reflect on what my life could have been if I had not won a literal lottery to get into a charter K-8 school across town. It was because of that blind luck that I was able to have a chance at a decent education and move away from any predestined doom based solely on my zip code.

I stuck out like a sore thumb at the school—my clothes were all too big, and I was one of only four students getting subsidized lunches—but it was an opportunity that was impossible to take for granted. The hour-long bus ride that I took nearly every morning for nine years was a reminder of how far I would have to go and how hard I would have to work to get out of the ghetto. I worked very hard and was accepted into the best public high school in the country.

Lowell High School was far from a breeze, but I graduated. Only three kids my age on my street graduated from high school, and I was the only one who went to college. By attending and graduating from UC Berkeley, which had always been a seemingly unattainable goal for a poor colored kid from the ghetto, I beat the odds. Of course, I worked supremely hard to get where I am today, but I cannot discount just how far good luck has gotten me. The prevailing sentiment that I have come away with is that I could have turned left one day instead of right and might very well have ended up still back at home, never having graduated, or perhaps even dead. When I look at how the others of my generation from my neighborhood faired, with many either in gangs, on drugs, or deceased, that thought is far from hyperbole. While I still say in a self-deprecating manner that I am a poor colored kid from the ghetto, it is because of my educational opportunities and a few instances of good luck that I have become just a little bit more than that.

Note from Ann: *While this essay breaks the rule about focusing on post–high school achievements, the decision was made to present the story in this way because the client's résumé and LORs focused extensively on his post-graduation work experience, and his addendum explained very low grades due to his need to work while in college. So providing this context was important in his personal statement. He approached the topic of his obstacles with tremendous humility. Some of the best personal statements are introspective and thoughtful and reflect on the societal factors and internal factors that made people who they are today. This applicant is currently attending Loyola Chicago.*

Cultural Identity

"Wait, you're from Paraguay? But aren't you Jewish?"

"Yes."

"There are Jews there?"

This is a variation of a conversation that I often have when I first meet people. The answer is, yes, there are Jews in Paraguay, but it is unclear for how much longer.

When I was six months old, my parents left behind a life rich with a large family, Sunday barbeques, afternoon coffees, and constant celebrations. However, it was clear to them that the Jewish community was slowly disappearing. The two synagogues and the one school were struggling to stay open, and intermarriage was becoming the norm. Our Jewish heritage and traditions were extremely important to my mother and father as they started a family. They were faced with the decision between staying with their families to enjoy the present and leaving them behind to build a new home for the future.

The brave young couple chose the hard route. They left behind a life of family support, of live-in maids and nannies, and of familiarity. In exchange, they found themselves with a small apartment, working long hours with nights spent moonlighting and, most of all, lonely. My parents made every effort to ensure that their sacrifices resulted in positive opportunities for me and for my younger sister. We maintained close ties with our families back in Asuncion, saving the time and money to visit every summer. I loved being able to spend time with my grandparents, my cousins, and my aunt and uncles. As I grew older, I noticed the deteriorating state of the Jewish school my parents had attended and that my cousins were attending. I saw the struggle to find even one rabbi to bring to the only Conservative synagogue. I saw the poverty on the streets and the true lack of a future.

Back in Miami, I appreciated the growing Jewish life. From a young age, my parents worked hard so that I could attend a Jewish preschool. We became members of a synagogue, and, slowly, but surely, our family began to build our own community, our home away from home. Throughout my education, I particularly took to learning about the histories of different people and cultures and how the world came to be how it is today. I wanted to understand my background and its importance. I enjoyed my history and civics lessons in middle school, taking the time to understand the laws I read about and the reasons behind them.

When I enrolled at the University of Florida, there was no doubt in my mind that I would continue to advance my studies with a political science major. I read new books, was introduced to different theories, and learned about the histories and complexities of different peoples both in the United States and around the globe. I learned more about my own roots by taking courses in Middle Eastern and Israeli studies, which exposed me to viewpoints very different from those that I had always known. For the first time, the values and outlook I had always been taught were not repeated back to me. Rather, I was encouraged to do the research and form arguments to support and articulate my beliefs as a supporter of Israel. Furthermore, I connected with the other side of my background with a course in Latin American and migration studies, in which I learned about the different ways that people from all around Latin America attempt to migrate to the United States.

As I read about and discussed American policies, I thought about my own family and what it meant to us to be able to migrate. I watched film documentaries about the hardships of migrants. I heard the arguments of those who opposed continued migration and discussed every side of the issue. The subjects that define my background are not ones with easy solutions, and they have taught me to listen to others and to form well-researched and respectful responses, skills that will aid my studies in law school.

In addition to a world of reading and theories, I decided to expand my education into something that I was not as familiar with. I joined the university's college of journalism and communications as a public relations double major. The goal was to enhance my skills by improving my writing and communication abilities, while meeting new people and experiencing a different kind of academia. This has been one of the best decisions I have made in my undergraduate career. My professors in this major have challenged me to work in real professional settings, do firsthand research, reach out to people in the community and work with new teams of peers. Public relations has allowed me to put my analytical skills to use in a way that will only benefit my future schooling and legal practice.

Still, there was one thing missing in my education. I have grown up speaking Spanish at home and have always been a fluent speaker, but I felt that I lacked a real education in writing, grammar, and literature. So finally, I decided to add a Spanish minor to my degree. In doing so, I have improved my Spanish skills immensely and feel comfortable writing and presenting in my family's native language. I am proud to tell my grandparents about this and to always remind myself of the importance of one's background, especially in an increasingly globalized and complex world. We are not a nation of only English speakers. Today, even school and government forms are available in multiple languages, and my fluency will expand my opportunities to work with more people on a wider range of projects.

Throughout my studies and increased connection with my heritage, I have become genuinely excited to learn about the law. I have learned about different cultures, people, histories, and governments. I have learned how to write and how to deliver an effective and persuasive presentation. What I still want, though, is a real understanding of the law and the way that it governs our societies and the way we live. While I remain undecided about my future practice, I have a special interest in international law and immigration law. I strive to be able to continue to take what I have learned from my past and apply it not only toward my own future, but also to the futures of others who are affected by these issues.

Note from Ann: *This essay is a good example of when to use identity as a personal statement topic rather than a diversity statement. The applicant is not writing about an obstacle overcome or a challenge, but rather about how her identity shaped her, how she took initiative to be educated about issues relating to her identity that she was previously sheltered from, and how she changed and grew through this experience. This was written by an applicant who was still in college.*

Overcoming Obstacles

Although I spent most of my high-school years homeless, without a room to call my own, I took full advantage of the excellent schools that surrounded me. I firmly believed that all of those late nights spent studying in strangers' garage apartments, second homes, church basements, and spare bedrooms would somehow pave the way for a brighter future. I viewed school as an equalizer. The formula was simple: do well in high school in order to attend college. I did not know why I wanted to go to college, besides the fact that successful people seemed to do it.

I focused on education simply as my one and only way out of poverty, until, in my junior year of high school, I first visited our nation's capital through the Close-Up Foundation. My life was inexorably changed. It was the first time I felt passionate about something that I believe truly mattered. Hearing policy debates and visiting the Supreme Court energized me. I fell in love with political theory and the ideals trumpeted in campaigns and found a level of comfort and satisfaction within the American political system, which inspired me to eventually major in political science.

In college, I wholeheartedly immersed myself in my studies. I loved debating, analyzing, and critically examining how politics might one day make this nation great again, or at least provide more opportunity for those in need. Many times it was difficult to openly debate with my classmates the merits of food stamps, disability assistance, or subsidized housing, but I felt it was important that I speak up, even if the class did not, could not, possibly understand. More often than not, the consensus of my peers swung against me, but my voice was heard.

I knew law school was in my future, but first I wanted to help other children realize that education could be key to changing their lives. I felt compelled to join Teach for America to help mitigate the educational performance gap between the rich and the poor. I knew, on a very personal level, that educational prospects are still largely determined by where you live and not ability or effort.

When I first entered my classroom, I was petrified. I was working in an alternative school for overage, under-credited students. The stakes were high and the task difficult, but I had overcome adversity in the past, and I was adamant that teaching would not be the exception. Despite my best intentions and the accumulation of sleepless nights, my classroom management and the quality of instruction suffered. I knew that I needed support, and I worked with my principal to create a Performance Improvement Plan (PIP), which outlines a tangible set of goals and expectations for the remainder of the year.

Slowly, but surely, I grew more confident in my teaching, but "good" and "great" were not yet adjectives at my disposal. Eight weeks later, my principal announced that I achieved the goals in my PIP and renewed my contract, but a twist grouped me among the faculty who, due to budgetary restrictions, were transferred to another school. I was assigned to Baltimore Talent Development High School, where I initially struggled to build a rapport with my students. However, my mind-set changed with an unexpected gift and some unsolicited country wisdom: I received a package containing a beautiful pair of square-toed leather cowboy boots and a handwritten note in which my father scrawled, "There never has been a horse that can't be rode or a cowboy that can't be throwed." I framed the note and put it on my desk, but it served as much more than a reminder of home and my father's generosity. I now fully understood that there was no golden bullet, magic unit plan, or deus ex machina principal to save me. I was on my own and had to accept responsibility and learn from my setbacks. In other words, I had to cowboy up.

Ultimately, I learned that leadership is not about taking the first step, it is about taking the next step, for only failure can improve your resiliency. I failed, spectacularly at some points, but my classroom environment eventually transformed, and the class reading-level average grew by over two years. It was through this experience that I learned that I had limits, and, no matter how tough my life had been, the world did not owe me anything. I not only learned that work ethic does not always translate to success at first, but I also learned that the resiliency I have developed over the course of my life, as well as the ability to ask for help and learn from my setbacks, are what set me apart and allowed me to be successful.

Note from Ann: *This applicant did a beautiful job of using his disadvantages to show his motivations for gaining an education and helping others to do so. He is walking the walk of helping others to overcome similar circumstances. He is currently attending Duke University School of Law.*

Artistic

In "The Schuyler Sisters," one of the hit songs from the groundbreaking musical *Hamilton*, the cast proclaims, "*Look around, look around at how lucky we are to be alive right now! History is happening in Manhattan, and we just happen to be in the greatest city in the world.*" When I think about my college experience and the process of deciding to apply to law school, this line resonates. Outside of class, I have spent most of my time in a theater or in an office supporting a theater. Theater has been a passion and a major part of my life for years, but my desire to become an entertainment attorney is much more rooted in what is happening today, rather than a reflection of my past experiences.

Today, in "the greatest city in the world," the theater industry is making history. Roundabout Theatre Company brought *She Loves Me* onto live stream. Deaf West's *Spring Awakening* made Broadway accessible to those with hearing disabilities. *Hamilton* was awarded sixteen Tony nominations, and it is grossing just as much money per week as shows that have been running for over a decade. These milestones and shows like *Hamilton* are the reason why I feel that this is the most important era to enter the theater industry and be part of its revolution.

Not only have shows like *Hamilton* dominated Broadway in terms of artistry and economics, but they have also begun to redefine the industry as a whole. For instance, *Hamilton* was reported for a controversial casting call that was inconsistent with Actors' Equity policy. Part of the power of *Hamilton* is that it purposefully casts actors with multicultural backgrounds in all roles but one (King George). They have specifically asked for "nonwhite" actors to audition, which shows how *Hamilton* seeks to change society's expectations. *Hamilton* is also timely: its political themes and messages have contributed to inspiring the younger generation to vote and have been the motivation behind many sponsored performances, such as the Hillary Clinton fund-raiser that occurred in July. *Hamilton* is bringing theater to the center of conversation and proving that theater serves a much greater purpose than what happens on the stage. Becoming an attorney would allow me to be a part of these victories and a community that is making waves all around us. Whether I am working with Actors' Equity on performers' rights or contributing to a singular production, I would have the opportunity to be directly involved in the decisions and processes that occur behind the scenes and consequently contribute to the movement that is reimagining the industry today.

Though producing shows and working with Broadway companies has formed this opinion and my decision to apply to law school, the cultural impact and innovation occurring behind shows like *Hamilton* have encouraged me the most to work hard and continue to pursue an education. Studying advertising and immersing myself in professional experiences in marketing and technology taught me how decisions are made, how big ideas come to life, and how determined leaders, like attorneys, are desperately needed to ensure that the show can succeed. None of the campaigns or productions can be imagined without numerous contracts, copyright protection services, and business negotiations. In the midst of learning and experiencing this for myself, I found that I become most passionate when I know that my work has had a direct impact on the overall success of a production. When reflecting on how

I loved managing $20,000 budgets as a producer, helping to coordinate Broadway cast announcements with the press, or the rush I felt when I would make seven-figure sales predictions for *Les Misérables,* this all makes sense. The idea of being able to work on influential shows while fulfilling my passions for the theater business and creating big ideas is what is driving me to pursue this educational experience.

Note from Ann: *We sort of broke a rule here by including a quote, but it wasn't meant to be inspirational or to set the tone for the essay, but to set up the timeliness of the topic—with Hamilton at the height of its fervor at the time. This applicant was trying to show why her motivations to be involved with the arts were relevant to her decision to study law and her interest in being in New York. She went on to conclude by talking about why she wanted to stay in New York, and the contacts she has made there, and how she hopes to continue her involvement in Broadway during law school. She accepted a full scholarship to New York University School of Law.*

Military

The summer before my senior year of high school was supposed to be the most enjoyable of my life. I had enlisted in the US Navy and would be spending my next summer in boot camp. I was excited about that upcoming adventure for a lot of reasons but most importantly because I'd have a way to pay for college since my family couldn't afford it. This excitement was short lived though, when a few weeks into the summer, my father abandoned my mother, my three siblings and myself. I wouldn't hear from him again for more than fifteen years. My focus shifted to helping my family.

All of a sudden, at the age of seventeen, I was the man of the house. I got a job at a fast-food restaurant and continued to work throughout my last year of high school. Unfortunately, it wasn't enough, and my childhood home was foreclosed on. We moved into a tiny two-bedroom apartment, my two brothers and I in one room and my mother and sister in another. Despite my mother's pleading for me not to, I dropped out of high school and got a full-time job working on air-conditioning units. Unfortunately, the navy would not take a high-school dropout and voided my enlistment contract. Working on air-conditioning units was honorable work, but it wasn't what I wanted to do for the rest of my life. Fortunately for me, this all took place in 1994, one of the greatest economic booms in our country's history. The navy was struggling to meet recruiting goals and temporarily allowed those without high-school diplomas to join if they scored high enough on the military entrance exam. Thankfully, my score qualified, and I was shipped off to boot camp shortly after.

I was focused on learning what it took to succeed in the military so that I could get promoted; getting promoted meant more money to help my family. I figured out right away that the navy didn't care about race, religion, sexual orientation, my background, etc. I was going to be judged on one thing: do I contribute to my unit? I learned quickly that the best skill I could develop was a strong work ethic. It was simple; if I worked hard, I'd get promoted. The military noticed and promoted me quickly. I was able to rise to the highest rank an enlisted person can attain significantly faster than the normal career progression. Today, my military pay grade is E9, and I am at the pinnacle of a military career: I am the command master chief of an F-18 Hornet squadron in the world's most powerful navy. It doesn't get any better than that for a career military person.

So here I sit, writing this statement onboard a US Navy Aircraft Carrier in the middle of the Pacific Ocean, participating in a twenty-three-nation joint exercise. I am at the highest level of the military chain of command, making six figures, with the admiration of family, friends, colleagues, and my community—why would I give that up for law school? While taking a leadership course at the Naval War College in 2011, I participated in a personal development exercise that explored the question, "If I could do anything right now, regardless of the obstacles, what would it be?" My answer was work to help military members and civilians impacted by war. After serving during three presidential administrations over my twenty-year career (Bill Clinton, George W. Bush, and Barack Obama) and participating in wars during each administration (Kosovo, Iraq, and Afghanistan), I've seen many of the positive effects of those three conflicts. However, I've also seen the gruesome and negative impacts, sometimes caused by those we were fighting, and unfortunately, occasionally caused by us. I began researching humanitarian and human rights law, and I knew right away that was what I was passionate about. Properly administered and enforced humanitarian and human rights law at an international level could have prevented many of the negative things I saw.

I have the luxury of attending law school virtually debt free due to the GI Bill, Yellow Ribbon Program, and receiving a military pension and medical coverage. I don't have to worry about a big salary; I am financially secure without a job. I get to pursue a career in humanitarian and human rights law that isn't bound by salary or the need to pay back student loans.

During my first ten years in the military, I put my two brothers through auto mechanic trade and journalism school and my sister through graphic design school. I feel thankful every day that I was able to help my siblings go to school and work in careers they love. That is, without question, my proudest accomplishment. I now hope to do the same for myself by attending law school.

Note from Ann: *This is a great example of how to use childhood experiences as context for a later decision. Don't you get to know this applicant throughout the essay, and aren't you impressed with his journey without him sounding arrogant? Rather, he sounds like the kind of guy you'd like to grab a beer with, right? And he does this without trying too hard. This essay is also a great example of how important voice is in an essay. By the way, this client is about to graduate from Georgetown University Law Center.*

Focusing on a Single Experience

A few hours after my fourth flat tire of the day, I was being handed the keys to a seedy motel room somewhere in the Pine Barrens of New Jersey. Exhausted and defeated, I rolled my packed-down bicycle into the room and I stood in front of the mirror, questioning my decision to complete a five-thousand-mile solo bicycle trip from Jersey City, New Jersey to Astoria, Oregon.

Turning away from self-doubt, I began to feel grateful. I had turned thirty years old a couple of months prior. I was unhappy in my job. This was the challenge I had longed for on those lonely, 4 a.m. subway rides home from a bartending shift: the chance to exceed the expectations of everyone, including myself, and to simultaneously find truth and purpose in that struggle. The next morning when I woke, I pointed myself west and never looked back.

The series of maps I'd spent months collecting, and the route they suggested, which at times seemed like a bunch of arbitrary twists and turns, would eventually have me riding through places that not only made me love and better understand America through its beauty but also forced me to take a hard look at some of our nation's not-so-celebrated decisions and the impacts that these policies have had on communities. The people in these communities had been abandoned by companies, by the dismantling of unions, and by the American government, despite having given their entire lives to working for them. They deserved better. Despite this, the people I encountered, whether from the hills of Kentucky or the farms of the Kansas plains, are some of the kindest and most generous people I have ever met. Their generosity and spirit shook the previously ingrained ideas of how I interacted with the world.

An important thing I learned from waking up every day and pedaling west was that every single day along that journey was different and nothing was guaranteed. I had no control over the weather, the grade of the road, or the austerity of the environment. The only thing that was guaranteed to me every morning, as I packed up my tent and stretched my sore legs, was that the entire day that lay ahead of me was going to be filled with purpose. It was going to be chocked full of the kind of pure, unadulterated, and genuine purpose that most people yearn for and yet rarely find in their daily lives. I was replete with gratitude. As long as I continued to give maximum effort, every single day that I moved in the right direction was, itself, a victory. The truth I discovered about myself, pedaling through the stifling heat that permeates the Blue Ridge Mountains in August or as I shook the snow off my tent that had accumulated overnight in Montana in late September or as I wiped the tears from my face the moment I caught a glimpse of the Pacific Ocean in October, was that I deeply desired this kind of purpose.

When I reached Astoria I took a few pictures of my bicycle posing in the foreground of the expanse of the Pacific Ocean, called my family, and quickly found myself sitting in a Chinese restaurant, dumbfounded, and waiting for a friend en route from Portland to pick me up.

I struggled, and continue to struggle, to accurately encapsulate the trip and its impact on me as a person to this day. In the weeks and months that followed my return home, my tan lines began to fade, but that longing for daily purpose and the memories of the inspiring people I met remained a part of me. I became obsessed with our nation's labor history and the struggle for worker's rights because of the time I spent in the depressed, yet hauntingly beautiful mountains of Kentucky. In Kansas, I was welcomed into a farmer's home for dinner, and we discussed the impacts of immigrant labor on their local farming communities. In Wyoming, I saw life on an Indian reservation, and I was deeply affected by how our nation's policy of exclusion has shaped the future of a people. These experiences, and my deep desire for purpose, led me to pursue my degree at Rutgers in a field where I felt I could make a difference, do the right thing, and achieve victories for the rights of workers.

As a federal investigator with the US Equal Employment Opportunity Commission, I have learned it is paramount to always begin with empathy and humility. As a US Army officer, I have learned to never quit and to find deep purpose in the call to fight in service of those who cannot fight for themselves. Something I hope to bring to the table as a student of the law is the ability to fearlessly accept great and seemingly impossible challenges and the ability to step back, find truth and purpose in the struggle, and look at my country and community with nothing but love in my heart.

Note from Ann: *This client's military experience and professional work experience were thoroughly covered in his résumé and his letters of rec, and his education and academic ability were illustrated by good grades after his military experience and an addendum that explained his early rocky start to college. Here, he got to show off his writing abilities and tell a story that showed he isn't all about doing something because it's impressive, that he appreciates and seeks out personal enrichment by hearing the stories of others, that he doesn't shy away from a challenge, and that these are all attributes that will assist him in the practice of law.*

Using a Motif/Theme

On a blustery winter day during my sophomore winter term, I received an unexpected package. I hurried up the steps of my dorm room, brimming with excitement, and soon enough the mystery was solved; inside lay a copy of *The Graduate* manuscript, accompanied by a hand-written note from the writer of the screenplay, Buck Henry. It was his last copy, reserved for his most adoring fan.

———

My connection to the film was immediate, occurring during my first viewing in high school. Ever since, it has held profound meaning in my life, although the reasons have developed through the years. At first, I interpreted the film as a coming-of-age love story, and—admittedly—when I met Mr. Henry at a campus event, that is how I expressed my connection to the film. It was only after I graduated and rewatched the film from this new perspective that I pieced together a deeper layer of the film's message: it was not a contemplative narrative on romance but a cautionary tale on self-exploration. The protagonist was too quick to find his sense of purpose in someone else; he fixated his energy on searching outside, rather than within, to shape his identity. Viewed through this lens, I identified a pivotal yet subtle message in the final moments of the film: they suggest that by tying his sense of purpose to another person, the protagonist's redemption may only be temporary.

———

In the months following my graduation, I felt myself pursuing a future in law without taking time for introspection. As much as I connected with the protagonist's crossing into adulthood, I did not want to become a similar casualty of impulse. I had spent over fifteen years pursuing excellence as a competitive tennis player and, in doing so, identified myself primarily through my athletic spirit. After leaving this tennis career on the courts of Hanover, I realized that I needed time to understand who I was after athletics. I also needed space away from philosophy and jurisprudence, my primary areas of study. Even though I loved the subjects—they allowed me to discover my fascination with how laws structure society and how legal actors weave together principles with a nuanced understanding of society and human behavior—they were the only subjects I had thus far studied so devotedly. I needed time to explore whether there were other areas on which I might want to focus my career.

I also wanted to discover my independence on another coast, away from tennis, away from the support of the classroom, and away from the comforts of home. Armed with these insights, I followed my interest in technology companies and moved cross-country to work at Square. By working directly with small businesses, learning their daily challenges, and often being the sole person responsible for onboarding high-profile clients, I gained an extensive understanding of how a young start-up evolves into a larger, more developed company.

Yet, I began to notice that—even in this setting—I gravitated toward the kinds of projects a lawyer would be attracted to: those of a theoretical nature, such as teaching myself the foundations of the payments landscape that Square helped to develop and, more directly, taking an interest in patent law by reading recent judicial opinions in my spare time. As my postgraduate introspection came full circle, my path toward law school blossomed. By heeding the lessons of *The Graduate* and taking time to be sure of my choices, I now appreciate that even though identities morph over time, true passions endure. My experiences after college uncovered this insight—in spending time away from law, I repeatedly came back to it. My own journey to find purpose brought a cross-country move and multiple work promotions. I open the next chapter of my life certain that my decision to pursue a career in law is one I have made with spirit, intent, and conviction.

Note from Ann: *This client's negative was a résumé that seemed scattered— she had a lot of interests that she pursued. This motif allowed her to discuss the ways in which she explored various interests and how she grew from each. She acknowledges that she lacked direction and explains how she ended up finding it. It talks about a story she is passionate about, and she makes it very personal. She could have written about her experiences as a college athlete, or working at a start-up post graduation, but this story allowed her to bring it all together in a way that didn't sound like a laundry list of everything she'd ever done. This client has been admitted to Columbia Law School and is currently on the waiting lists at both Harvard and Stanford Law Schools.*

Study Abroad

When most people think about Paris, the first thing that comes to mind is the Eiffel Tower or the chocolates in the shops on Rue Rivoli. But when I think about Paris, I think about the city that helped me grow and learn about myself and the world. In the just under five months that I spent there, I learned much more than the correct way to ask for dessert at dinner. Two and a half months before my arrival, terrorists executed the deadliest attack on Paris since World War II. Though I considered cancelling my trip, I realized that the experiences I would gain from living in a foreign country were too important to sacrifice just because there is malice in the world that takes the form of bombs and guns.

One of the most profound experiences that I had while in Paris—and really in life—was going to the first soccer game in Stade de France after the attack. I felt proud to be part of the moment when the French National Team won the game, and that experience showed me the importance of resilience. The stands were packed despite the four levels of security checks leading into the stadium. Each person was clearly so passionate about healing their country's wounds and making it feel whole again after facing such tragedy. In the face of evil and destruction, the people of France taught me to be brave and to be strong, especially in a time of hardship.

My grasp of the French language afforded me many opportunities during this time. After my first week there, I had great confidence in my conversational abilities and was able to converse with virtually every person I encountered. I was even able to form relationships with my local grocer and pastry shop owner. These relationships afforded me the ability to understand the community more deeply. Because I was in a different country while both Europe and the United States were volatile, I began to understand the significance of seeking out differing points of view before making decisions about my opinions. With each new headline, I would read the news in both the French and American media, and I would question why a headline on one side of the Atlantic had not reached the other. My innate ability to read French allowed me to have a deeper understanding of the people and the culture that I was attempting to assimilate into. Not only did the journalistic content and styles diverge in their portrayals of current events, but also the norms of what is acceptable to publish are greatly different. Since coming home, I have continued seeking out vastly different news media outlets with different political slants and ideologies to form my opinions. As a result of exposing myself to a variety of information, I am far more knowledge-able about current events. Moreover, and more importantly, I am more aware of how those around me may feel and am better able to work with those who do not share my views.

From paying special attention to current events, I was also able to notice more readily the differences in how the French people generate change. The way the French use their right to protest empowered me to make sure that my voice is heard in my community and to ensure that as many other people as possible are given an opportunity to be heard. The French as a society protest much more than the American people. The subway shuts down, the air traffic controllers go on strike, and even the teachers walk out of their schools. I experienced many different protests like these in Paris and around France. I saw people stand up for what they believed in and effectuate change within their government. Seeing these people, young and old, making a difference gave me a hope that I have not always found in the United States. For my whole life, my family has fought for my brother, who has Tourette's Syndrome. This has shaped my perception of representation and, com-bined with witnessing the French people successfully and productively protest, affirmed my desire to make sure that those who do not have a voice in society benefit from representation.

In my time abroad, I came to the surprising conclusion that I am proud of my religious identity. The French are widely known for being anti-Semitic. In the United States, I have never felt particular pride in my religion; however, walking through the Jewish quarter every day on my way to class and seeing the armed soldiers standing outside of the Jewish Art Museum left me feeling proud to be a young Jewish woman. I was, and continue to be, proud of my lasting religion, which has sur-vived centuries of discrimination and hate. I was proud to see the beauti-ful Hebrew mosaics on the walls and the lines for falafel going around the block. Seeing the guards reinforced this pride because I knew that, regardless of the persecution that continuously plagues my religion, we protect what is most important to us: family and traditions. Being Jewish became a salient part of my identity.

Because of these experiences, I realized that being a well-rounded human being requires careful reflection about the influence of place and the differences that exist between cultures. What I thought would be a semester spent traveling and excessively eating croissants morphed into a time of great contemplation about who I am and who I will strive to be. I want to be confident in my convictions, resolute in times of tragedy, well rounded in my views, and, most of all, proud of the person I have grown into.

Note from Ann: *As mentioned above, this essay broke my "no study abroad" rule. But, it gets across a learning experience, incorporates personal identity, and a changing consciousness of what that means, and also highlights her foreign language proficiency. This client will be attending Cardozo Law School.*

Older Applicant/Career Change

I was accepted into the Master's Program in Film and Television Production at the University of Southern California's School of Cinematic Arts right out of undergrad. It was a very exciting time for me, and the program was a fulfilling experience that taught me everything I have ever applied to the craft of filmmaking. What it didn't teach me was how to interact and deal with people and other business aspects of the industry. That's where experience had to come in.

Being from a small town in Indiana, one could say I was a little on the optimistic, or maybe even naïve, side of how people treat you. I believed in the classic Midwest work ethic and "treat people how you want to be treated" method. What you eventually find in the entertainment industry is that it can appear to be very unfair; in fact, it can seem downright mean. Often the work you find has little to do with creative talent at all. I know this probably does not seem surprising, but to my young self almost twenty years ago, I wasn't exactly prepared for the cutthroat and overly competitive nature of it.

I was a fortunate masters graduate in that I was represented by a high-profile talent firm right out of school. After several big meetings at studios, multiple screenings, and even more introductions (including to a new manager), I had my first opportunity to develop a feature script for theatrical release. I remember sitting on a white couch in the middle of a Beverly Hills mansion with an original copy of the classic film script *Some Like It Hot* lying in front of me on a marble coffee table. It was intimidating to say the least. The first thing the male producer said to me was that I was a lot younger than he thought I would be based on my student film, and he thought I would have been bald (as he was). Although this was a little awkward, I went with it and made a joke (after all, we were developing a comedy movie), the producers laughed (thank goodness), and the next thing I knew we were having major story conversations about the new script. As the husband-and-wife producer team argued about a story point, I was literally tackled by their two enormous, very friendly, black hound dogs. I have no idea what breed they were. What I do remember is that the only suit I owned at the time was covered in dog hair and saliva, and I was sweating from nerves. The whole experience was somewhat surreal, and the next thing I knew the male producer was on the phone with an executive from Artisan Entertainment, telling him that they had found their writer/director. There were three more meetings in that Beverly Hills mansion, all culminating in my clothes drenched in sweat, saliva, and dog hair.

You might be surprised to hear that in the end I didn't get the directing job; in fact, I eventually discovered that they were simply using me for guidance. I had spent a lot of time and effort on that project and was not compensated a cent for it. It was a hard lesson to learn and harder to take in my saliva-stained, hair-infested suit. Although my agent assured me that it was like this for all budding filmmakers—that I was simply paying my dues—it was around this time that I first started thinking about the concept of fairness and rights of artists in the industry. Why should anyone work for free in an industry that made so much money? That question stayed with me.

What I did learn from that experience and others is that the entertainment "business" is as hard, and maybe harder in some ways, than mastering the art forms that it utilizes to make money. It is hypercompetitive, and the rules are very blurry. I had heard back in my days at a local news station that one should be prepared to have your material stolen. It happened to me twice throughout my career. Part of this is due to how the system is set up. You have to put your neck out to get noticed, and this means that often you have to work for free.

At the same time, the industry was changing drastically. There was a major shift toward digital, and the implications of this were bigger than those two large hounds I encountered in Beverly Hills. The Internet as a means of distribution opened up loopholes and blurred lines of communication and even creative credit. What constituted an original work anymore? People were downloading illegal copies of music (remember Napster) and movies and plagiarizing at an alarming rate. The "business" of entertainment was struggling to keep up with this new global phenomenon.

The business that I worked so hard to get a foot into had literally changed overnight. Media and cable conglomerates were gobbling up movie studios and television networks. I was fortunate at the time to cross over from being just an artist in the film and television industry to a business "creative" in the dominant media and communications industry. It was a natural fit given my marketing and creative background. It was here where I learned both how creativity fit into the industry and the business end of the communications industry as well. The summary of all my hard-earned experiences naturally led to the formation of my own creative business. I now develop creative for business owners while helping them navigate through the very complicated, modern advertising landscape. I have found that the aspect of helping people is a source of great fulfillment.

Of course, the same questions I thought about after my first Hollywood development meeting come up time and time again with clients, especially with regard to rights and legalities of content. The artist in me always harks back to that first meeting and its implications. Given what is going on in the world today with Apple Music, Google, and other giant corporations, I believe there is a need for someone to step up to protect those rights. Experience can be a huge help.

Note from Ann: *This applicant does a good job of covering a lot of ground in a compelling way, explaining why he entered the industry, what he learned, and addressing the question of why he would apply to law school in his forties. It shows career growth and that he thinks about situations and projects and isn't just motivated by titles.*

Extracurricular Activity

"You're doing your job all wrong, man. The point of this team is to travel and drink, especially as the man in charge."

When I joined the Model UN travel team in my first year, the University of Virginia was barely cracking the top fifty teams in the nation. Once I was elected as the Inter-Collegiate Coordinator (ICC), I made considerable changes to the team, specifically expanding its membership to allow more delegates to participate. Instead of selecting the top members of the team from the outset of the school year, we allowed more students to compete, which helped them develop their skills throughout the year.

To proactively demonstrate the results that our team could achieve through this new strategy, I began revamping our conference schedule strategically. This involved striking a balance between larger and smaller conferences, ensuring that our delegates could gain experience competing against a wealth of other delegates and garner the university some much-needed wins. With my vision in mind, I instituted a new training program that involved a number of meetings before competitions, encompassing activities to practice researching, directive-writing, crisis note-writing, and public speaking. I noticed that as the team grew closer and more unified, we were able to not only foster a genuine sense of community but also experience more success in conferences.

All of this did not come without pushback; UVA had a reputation on the Model UN circuit of being the "fun team," and many of the older members were both proud of this reputation and intent on perpetuating it. One such alumnus who was appalled by my endeavors responded with the comment at the top of this essay. Focusing on the goal of organizational success allowed me to persevere through this repudiation by framing difficult decisions in terms of what advanced my team best. The notoriety we gained on the circuit for our vast improvements incentivized other teams to travel to the conference that the University of Virginia hosts, which then fed back into our budget to allow the team to travel more frequently.

Galvanized by my ability to bring successes to the Model UN team, I ran for philanthropy chair of my fraternity the following semester. We were coming off a series of years in which our philanthropy events not only failed to meet fund-raising goals, but also lost money for the fraternity. I was determined to change this trajectory and make our philanthropy events "profitable" again. Thus, I initiated the "All You Can Eatsters" event to benefit the Judy Fund of the Alzheimer's Association, in which we solicited food donations from local Charlottesville restaurants and hosted a buffet at a flat cost for attendees.

This event involved a lot of personal legwork, but my biggest struggle consisted of combatting the general lethargy of the other brothers in the fraternity. Despite the hours I dedicated to the project and how little responsibility I put on their shoulders, they demonstrated a complete unwillingness to comply with even the simplest of requests, including attending the event itself. It can be disheartening when others in your organization do not share the same enthusiasm about your projects; it is humiliating when others hold no regard for the time and effort dedicated to a cause. I became increasingly detail driven as the event neared, to the degree that I lost sight of why I initiated this project in the first place: the cause itself. I reframed my goals to focus on improvement from the previous years rather than arbitrary fund-raising benchmarks. Ultimately, attendance was much greater than expected, and all the food was consumed in under two hours. After the end of the event, in addition to donations that were solicited throughout a month-long period, the event raised over $6,000 for the Judy Fund.

My drive to improve the organizations that I join applied in my legal internship this summer as I balanced multiple projects and worked across departments. My work forced me to further refine my organizational abilities and convinced me that the skills I learned as an undergraduate would allow me to succeed in the legal profession. I look forward to using what I will learn in law school to continue to give back to the organizations that matter to me and to the profession as a whole in meaningful ways.

Note from Ann: *This is a great example of how you take an activity from college that is considered fairly typical for a prelaw applicant and make it interesting and thoughtful and use it to demonstrate personal characteristics beyond "I'm great at oral arguments!" It shows passion and enthusiasm and a drive to make something better and how he grew from this experience. It's a good direction for someone who is a traditional college applicant lacking significant work experience. This client will be attending New York University School of Law (where he applied binding).*

Parting Thoughts

I hope that these examples show you that you don't have to write the most memorable and impressive story ever written to have an impactful, effective law school personal statement. My intention is to show you that authenticity and thoughtfulness go a long way. Keeping the focus on you, your experiences, your motivations, and your personal growth is always the right direction for your personal statement.

Key Takeaways

- Personal statements should be authentic, rather than unique.
- Emphasize strengths, including growth and maturity.
- There should be some relation to your choice to study law and/or qualities you bring to the legal profession.
- Follow each school's prompt and requirements.

CHAPTER 10

DRAFTING OPTIONAL ESSAYS

Should You Submit an "Optional" Essay?

Many law schools provide opportunities to submit a second essay (and even a third) with their applications. Sometimes it's a "Diversity Statement," and sometimes it's referred to as an optional essay and a prompt is provided. My rule of thumb is that, if an optional essay applies to your situation and does not repeat your personal statement, then you really should do the essay, even if a school says that your admission chances won't be impacted should you choose not to do it. Not only does the essay provide you with an opportunity to show something new about yourself, but it's also a way to show you really are interested in the school because you went the extra mile in your application to create something just for them.

Below is an explanation of some typical topics for optional essays.

Diversity

Be careful here because there are two kinds of diversity statements. One asks about obstacles overcome. The other asks about how you will add to the diversity of the law school.

These are very different questions. Why? Because lots of people add diversity, and fewer people have faced obstacles because of their diversity. If you are the child of immigrants who came to this country penniless and shared a one-bedroom apartment with six family members while you were growing up, and your non-English-speaking parents washed dishes at the Chinese restaurant as their second jobs at night, then you probably are familiar with obstacles and with overcoming them.

If you are from a culturally diverse background, but grew up in a privileged environment, and never faced any discrimination, you can probably write a good essay about learning from two different cultures, but only the second essay prompt applies to you. See the difference?

Everyone has a gay best friend or a friend who is Muslim: please don't write about someone else's struggle and try to get points for empathizing or appreciating the struggles of others. This can be especially tricky when we are talking about your parents' struggles. You need to bring the story around to you and your life rather quickly. This is your law school application, and it must be about you. If you wrote about your struggles as a minority or as a single mother in your personal statement, don't repeat those things here. However, you may decide to use your personal statement as your diversity statement and write your personal statement on something entirely different for schools that provide the option of both essays.

Other experiences may be responsive to a diversity prompt, including going back to school as an older student, military experience, sexual orientation, growing up abroad, speaking other languages, a difficult family background, socioeconomic disadvantage, being the first in your family to attend college, and religious identity. Like with the personal statement, it's not about being unique. Don't worry that other people have been through similar struggles. Instead, focus on your experiences and how they have shaped you.

If you don't have a compelling idea for a diversity statement topic, *don't submit one!* More is not necessarily better. "Do not include minor speed bumps such as not winning a school organization election, or coming in last in your swim meet once as a major obstacle you have overcome," says Dean Lennon. Submitting a story along these lines will demonstrate that you lack not only diversity but also self-awareness and that a number of your peers have faced obstacles in their lives.

Examples of Diversity Statements
Race

When telling the story of my life, much attention must be paid to my difficult relationship with race. With a Japanese mother and a black father, I became acutely aware of race and racism at an early age and have dealt with it all my life in ways both unique to mixed people and often ignored by most non-mixed folks.

My first conflicts with race were within my own family. Even as a young child, my father impressed upon me the importance of knowing about and claiming my "blackness." At age five, I would proudly tell anyone who asked that I was African American. But then the Japanese part of me went ignored, much to the chagrin of my mother. I recall once when my mother asked me what my ethnicities were, and I said, "African American and...Chinese?" She was not particularly happy about that, as one might imagine.

Add my extended family into the mix, and you have a perfect situation for insensitive questions to be asked, like, "Why is he white?" and underhanded insults, for example, in reference to my father, "Well at least he has a job." Family reunions were often difficult for me, as I stuck out like a sore thumb in the midst of people who were supposed to be my "in-group"; I was too dark for the Japanese kids and too light for the black kids. This would prove to be indicative of my lifelong inability to find that automatic social group enjoyed by people with similar skin tones. I frequently felt isolated in social situations by never having that immediate recognition and acknowledgment that comes with a shared culture and history based on skin color.

My precollege years were filled with much of the same, but, for the first time, with a touch of real hatred. The majority of the population at my public high school was Chinese. On my very first day, after my first class, a Chinese student walked up to me and said, "You are responsible for the rape of my country." It was so out of the blue that I was left standing there dumbfounded as he walked away. The anti-Japanese sentiment did not end there. In fact, my best friend, then and now, and his friends, called me a Jap to my face at least a few times. Needless to say, it was all very difficult to face at such a young age, but I refused to be silenced and pushed aside simply for being different. Because most of the racism directed at me during high school was related to my being partially Japanese, I embraced that side of me, almost as an act of defiance against the paradigm of hatred and ignorance.

High school was the first time that I felt the weight of institutionalized racism as well. Not only did I have to deal with the racist Asians at my high school because I was the wrong kind of Asian, I also had to deal with being a little dark and having what amounted to an Afro. During my first year with a license, the daily morning routine consisted of me taking my father to work in the family car and then driving to school. I quickly learned that taking the scenic route through the city was not ideal, as I was pretty routinely followed and stopped by the police for being a suspicious black teenager in parts of town where there should not be any blacks. I was not anywhere near to being Rodney King, and I certainly was not being attacked by police dogs or fire hoses, but I was not a terribly long way off from wanting to march in the streets and blast *Fuck the Police* from my car radio.

While my ethnic heritage has presented speed bumps along the road, I would be disingenuous in the retelling of my story if I claimed my ethnicities as a hindrance to the development of my character. My wife and I recently took a trip to Taiwan. She had been before, but it was my very first time out of the country, so I was excited to experience all the beauty and idiosyncrasies of new culture. My wife was quick to point out the many differences between "them" and "us," from the very orderly lines at the subway stations to the obvious ethnic homogeneity. But, after spending a few days there, and talking to several locals in broken Mandarin, all I could see were similarities between the Taiwanese and everyone else I had ever met: everyone had the same struggles and the same desires. Everyone had bills to pay, loved ones to care for, and dreams for the future. This first trip out of the country made me realize that while I may have had many difficulties throughout my life because of my mixed ethnic heritage, I have developed into a richer citizen of the world because I see people for who they really are. Instead of focusing in on what sets people apart, I focus on what makes people similar, and that has helped me relate to many people from a diverse set of backgrounds.

Family Circumstances

My parents fought for years. My dad's drinking was a strain on my family for much of my childhood, and ultimately led to the ending of my parents' marriage. As the oldest of three, I felt a weight of culpability for the pain it caused my little brother and sister. Maybe it was because I had just begun high school as the divorce materialized, or maybe it's the inherent nature of the eldest sibling—but before long, I took on the role of leader of the family.

Before they actually separated, there were mornings when I'd ride to the local bar with my mom so that I could drive my dad's car back to the house. Sometimes, I'd come home from band practice to find my sister crying on the couch, and my dad passed out on the living room floor. There were nights when she'd cry on my shoulder while I finished writing a paper. My goal was always to show her strength in the only way I knew how: digging in and doing the best I could, in the classroom or practicing in the pool. Despite my mom's love and kindness, her attention was often pointed toward rehabilitating my dad and salvaging the marriage. At times it felt like I was the only parent in my family, but it was a role I embraced.

In a way, all of this became normal, and throughout high school, I threw myself into every activity I could—on the one hand, as a way to cope with my family falling apart around me and, on the other, to show my brother and sister resolve during a time of uncertainty and pain. I swam on the high-school swim team, often practicing before school at 5 a.m. and after school until 7 p.m. Quite literally, there were days where I was lucky to see the sun, let alone feel it. I was a part of the marching band, becoming the drum major my senior year. I was on Academic Superbowl, took AP classes, was a class officer—I list these not just to demonstrate that I was involved, but to emphasize that school and everything about it became my haven, a safe-place of sorts. When I wasn't in the pool, on the field, or in the library, I was with my siblings. I'd sit at the foot of my sister's bed and quiz her on her vocabulary words or help her craft her history report. My brother joined the marching band with me when he reached high school, where we both thrived. Like me, he had found his safe-space.

My friends have joked for years that I act older than my age, frequently gifting me with "Happy 80th!" cards on my birthday. Back in middle school, these taunts used to irritate me. "Why would being mature be a bad thing?" I thought to myself. As I've had the time to reflect, what I now recognize is that the early maturity and responsibility that my family situation required was foundational to my outlook on life. Teenage heckling aside, I became a better person and leader because of it.

As I was a witness alongside my brother and sister to our family crumbling for years, I realized that what was within my power was the example I could set and the love I could provide. I couldn't mend a marriage or cure my dad's addiction, but I could do everything in my power to be a better brother and a better person. I wasn't perfect, and there were plenty of rough patches, but my siblings and I couldn't be closer and the experience shaped who we are today. I like to think that being a leader is a lot like being a brother, and in the many leadership positions that I've held, I've always attempted to hold myself to that standard: being the best role model I can, working as hard as I can, and loving with all my heart.

Identity

"¿Qué quieres?" It's a simple phrase—"what do you want?" Except, I can't roll my Rs, and my accent will never be quite right. My mother is the only person to ever say that my accent is good. She's lying, of course, and the majority of her side of the family takes turns making fun of the guera. By calling me "guera," they challenge my heritage; they call me "white" even though I am not. Our differences stem from more than just my poor Spanish-speaking abilities. When I was younger, I desperately wanted deep brown doe eyes like my abuelita. They were beautiful and held admiration and love, but most importantly they were what everyone had in common. Instead, I was stuck with eyes the color of boogers or "ojos del color de mocos" as my cousins loved to tease. Thankfully, I share the same dark curly hair that runs in the family; however, my skin tone is the lightest even though it's really only a tad paler than my mom's. My appearance makes me stick out, but the fact that I went to college makes me incredibly different. I come from a long line of farmers, laborers, and high-school dropouts (including my older brother). They look at me like an alien.

My family is traditional and Catholic. They're the kind of Catholics that see a rose and automatically think that Saint Thérèse has heard their prayers. I don't think belief in a higher power is a bad thing, but when people use it as a reason to hate, it inflicts extreme emotional damage. I only came out to my family as a lesbian a month after Pope Francis said, "If someone is gay and searches for the Lord and has good will, who am I to judge?" This singular sentence started a conversation in my family; this conversation revealed that my mom thought everyone should be welcome in church. My abuelita scrunched up her nose at the thought, before eventually settling on the idea that she loved Ellen DeGeneres, so of course, she should be welcome at church (which was close enough for me). It disturbed a few members of my family; they feared for the sanctity of marriage, did not want to see affectionate same-sex couples, and felt that the pope's sentence would encourage such a thing to occur more frequently. After I came out, my abuelita's eyes—which once held admiration and love—betrayed only sadness and fear. My mom's brown eyes followed suit. My cousins don't look me in the eye anymore, and they only ever speak Spanish when I'm around in hopes that I won't understand it—even though I do. I make a lot of my family members uncomfortable and, just recently, I've grown okay with that.

My mom and abuelita fear for the quality of life I'll lead; they constantly pray for me—not for me to change who I am—but for my life to go as smoothly as possible. It is their support that allowed me to truly love myself and to look at the things that make me different with a smile rather than a tear.

Financial Challenges

My mother not only embodied the value of hard work, she prioritized instilling it in her two sons. She understood from her own upbringing that if we were to succeed we would have to work hard. As a woman without much of a formal education on which to lean—or, frankly, a partner to support her for the first half of my childhood—she kept us together.

Ever since I was a small child, I learned the value and importance of doing more with less. No one could have modeled this better than my mother.

My mother would bartend nights to make sure we had what we needed. Looking back, I know it must have been a huge struggle, raising two boys with less than a high-school education with little support. She had dropped out of school when she was sixteen and received her GED at twenty-four, when pregnant with me. Yet, somehow, my mother managed to get both her boys through high school and college.

My life changed dramatically when my family moved to Port Norris in 1996. We left my grandmother's house, where my brother and I took care of chickens and rabbits on her small acre of land. When my mom remarried, they decided it was best to raise us on a farm, so they bought a twenty-five-acre plot, about thirty minutes away, in the next county. The farm was a tremendous amount of responsibility and, at the time, I didn't truly appreciate what it meant for me.

I will never forget graduating eighth grade, when our principal addressed the crowd and said, "Look at these students and guard them close, as only half of them will go on to graduate high school." At that time, I had to make a conscious decision to either go to Millville High School or Cumberland Regional High School (CRHS), which—while twenty-five miles from my house in the middle of a cornfield—would allow me to participate in the Future Farmers of America Program. I chose Cumberland because I love everything about agriculture: I was active in 4H, and I knew that I wanted a future working with the people who grew our food. The idea of going to a school that had a program around agriculture was very exciting to me, even if it meant getting up earlier to milk goats and water cows before getting on the school bus.

My passion for agriculture arose from the community in which I was raised. The average income for a family in New Jersey is roughly $87,000 dollars a year; in my community, the average family earns $42,000 a year. While New Jersey as a whole touts a bachelor's degree education for 36 percent of its residents over the age of twenty-five—7 percent higher than the national average—the rate for my community is 14 percent. It was very common for young people where I grew up to get involved with drugs. I remember being on free and reduced lunch throughout middle school and high school (along with nearly half my classmates). It was rural poverty: grocery stores were fifteen miles—a twenty-minute drive—from our house. We never had much money growing up, so my mom would regularly shop at thrift stores and value supermarkets. This was why the farm was a vital part of our upbringing: it made us a part of our own food system. It really came out of necessity.

My high-school years were tough—I would have to get up before school to take care of the animals; when I got home, I would spend a couple hours each night feeding and watering them. I would eat dinner, go out and milk the goats, and then do my homework. In the spring, when it was kidding season, I would stay up until one or two in the morning helping ewes and does give birth. On the weekends, we did bigger projects—fixing fencing, mowing pastures, building stalls. When my brother left for college, I had to pick up his chores. My parents asked me to not play basketball my junior year so that I could be home more, while my stepdad looked for a job because we were hurting for money.

From these experiences, I learned how to be a contributing part of a family. It made me understand the importance of food justice, as well as its impact on a community. My upbringing inspired me to commit to helping others and motivated me to become a public servant. I understand the importance of dedication, sacrifice, passion, and hard work.

Why *THIS* Law School?

This question has been increasingly popular on law school applications: the University of Pennsylvania, the University of Michigan, Tulane Law School, University of California, Irvine, and Loyola University Chicago are among the schools that ask for an "optional" essay about your interest in their school. Why is it important that you are interested in the school? Because of "yield protection." What is this? Schools are ranked, largely, upon their admission criteria and their acceptance rates. Law schools are very protective of these numbers as a result. Therefore, they don't want to hand out acceptances to people who they feel are unlikely to attend. This is why people with very strong numbers are often waitlisted at schools that should be safety schools for them (I'm talking to you, Georgetown Law).

So, if a school asks you why you are interested, you need to show you've done some research. Most school websites are pretty thorough, especially if you look beyond the "Prospective Student" pages and really explore the activities of the faculty and students. Here are some things to think about mentioning:

- any specific ties you have to the school (friends who are at the law school, parents who attended, a supervisor who is a graduate) or to the area (your parents moved there recently, etc.);
- the similarities (collegial atmosphere, college town versus urban atmosphere, etc.) between that campus and your college campus (assuming you've been successful in that environment in the past);
- a particular focus of the law school (that you are sure is real and active and substantial) that matches with a specific interest that is evident from your activities such as an environmental or immigration law clinic that corresponds with volunteer efforts you've done in the past;
- that you have met with someone at the law school or visited the school; and
- if you are applying for the part-time program, explain why this is the right fit for you so that they do not think you are applying to that program because of a perception that it is easier to get in.

Here are some things to avoid mentioning:

- claiming that a school's environmental law program is the reason you are applying when there is nothing in your background to show any connection to environmental issues;
- mentioning a summer study abroad program as your reason for applying because you can (generally) participate in any law school's study abroad program no matter where you attend; and
- overly broad statements that could be applied to almost any law school (what I call "brochure text") such as "esteemed faculty" or "renowned faculty" or "national reputation" or "impressive bar passage rate," or "collegial atmosphere." Be more specific.

"Why Berkeley" Sample Essay

I am interested in Berkeley Law because its rigorous, interdisciplinary, and diverse environment is ideal for preparing me to tackle real-world challenges. I am particularly drawn to Berkeley's Social Justice and Public Interest specialization, the Center for Law and Technology, and the Samuelson Clinic.

In my current position as a program associate at the Philadelphia-based nonprofit Maternity Care Coalition (MCC), I have worked with the Programs and Public Policy departments to address issues facing pregnant women and families with young children. In my two years at MCC, I have developed a nuanced understanding of the social, economic, and legal challenges our clients face every day. Through the Social Justice and Public Interest specialization at Berkeley, I would build on this knowledge by taking courses such as Critical Race Theory and Topics in Reproductive Justice and by attending extracurricular events at the Thelton E. Henderson Center.

While the specialization in Social Justice and Public Interest law complements my professional experiences, the Center for Law and Technology complements my undergraduate education. As a neuroscience major in college, I developed a strong foundational understanding of the life sciences and a specialized understanding of the brain and nervous system. At Berkeley, I would use this training to participate in the BCLT's experiential learning opportunities, such as the IP Legal Assistance for Life Sciences Start-Ups program.

Most of all, I am interested in Berkeley Law because I would like to continue my career in social justice while incorporating my background in the sciences. The Samuelson Law, Technology and Public Policy Clinic aligns perfectly with this goal: it would give me the opportunity to develop critical legal skills, such as navigating relationships with clients and working with a legal team and to expand my experience with social justice issues pertaining to law and technology.

My background and professional experiences have equipped me with a solid foundation to address legal issues. Berkeley Law's specialized programs, experiential learning opportunities, and interdisciplinary approach make it the ideal place for me to use my existing skillset to contribute to the legal field.

Thoughtful Essays

The University of Pennsylvania and University of Michigan Law have optional essay topics that are fairly serious. For example, in the past, the University of Pennsylvania has offered the opportunity for applicants to respond to one or more of the following topics:

- Describe how your background or experiences will enhance the diversity of the Penn Law community (e.g., based on your culture, race, ethnicity, religion, sexual orientation, ideology, age, socioeconomic status, academic background, employment, or personal experience).

- Dean Michael A. Fitts has highlighted the core strengths that make Penn Law the best place to receive a rigorous and engaging legal education: genuine integration with associated disciplines; transformative, forward-looking faculty scholarship; highly regarded experiential learning through urban clinics and our pro bono pledge; innovative, hands-on global engagement; and a manifest commitment to professional development and collegiality. These are the qualities that define Penn Law. What defines you? How do your goals and values match Penn Law's core strengths?

- Describe a time when, as a member of a team, you particularly excelled or were especially frustrated. What was your role within that team? What was the outcome?

- If you do not think that your academic record or standardized test scores accurately reflect your ability to succeed in law school, please tell us why.

The last one is the easiest since it's basically the addendum you've already drafted for other schools to cover these topics, so don't just do that one and pat yourself on the back for doing optional essays. The first one is the diversity statement but trimmed to one page. The second is one that should be impossible to ignore: if you're trying to make the case that Penn is the right place for you, you should be able to answer this question. The team member topic has the potential to be done very well— I've seen good essays on this written by musicians as part of groups and also by applicants who worked in groups in an MBA program. It's pretty open-ended and gives you the chance to highlight a professional experience in a new way (The "team" essay is not the time to talk about your high-school football glory days). Remember to follow the directions and stick to the page limits provided by a school.

The Fun Essays

I love that Georgetown Law doesn't take itself too seriously. Here are the five optional essay topics they offered in 2017:

1. Who is your "one phone call" and why?
2. Write page 150 of your autobiography.
3. "Anyone who has never made a mistake has never tried anything new" (Albert Einstein). Describe your most interesting mistake.
4. Fill a 5.5″ long by 2.5″ wide box in any way you'd like.
5. Prepare a one-minute video that says something about you.

These questions can seem overwhelming if you think too hard about them. But if you try to get creative, these can be fun to attack. Of course, each essay is limited to 250 words, but think of that as a relief. It's only two paragraphs! Avoid talking about Mom and Dad in your one phone call essay—it feels really young and immature. Be creative with your autobiography—it can be something that hasn't yet happened! Show some personality with these essay topics and use every word wisely.

I've seen some great videos by those who dare. With planning and editing, you can say quite a lot in sixty seconds, and it definitely lets the viewer get to know you a bit more as a person. Show the video around to people before you submit it: make sure you don't speak too quickly, seem cocky, or fake or odd in some unexpected way and that your captions are error free.

The 250-Word Open-Ended Essay

Yale is famous for this one. My clients who have been admitted to Yale all used this essay to share something about themselves that would not have been evident elsewhere in the application. On shorter essays, really think about each word you choose to use. Avoid repetition. Get right to your point. Most importantly, know what your point is.

Key Takeaways

- If an optional essay topic applies to you, you should write it.
- When writing a school-specific essay, take the time to research the school.
- Diversity statements should focus on either an obstacle you overcame or how you identify yourself and would contribute to the diversity of a student body and/or of the legal profession.
- Adhere strictly to length requirements.

CHAPTER 11

DECIDING WHERE TO APPLY

There are three kinds of law school applicants:

1. Those who are geographically tied to a region.
2. Those who are hunting for the best law school that will take them.
3. Those who are looking for the best value.

People who fall into category number one have the easiest time choosing schools to apply to because there may be only one or two schools in their city. In this case, you want to make friends with the admission offices at the schools where you plan to apply. Make sure they know you, and make sure you attend events, visit the campus, and listen to whatever advice they give to you. Personal connection will matter, especially if your numbers are marginal.

Cost should be a driving factor in almost everyone's law school list. After all, you could use your trust fund to buy a house one day if you don't spend it all on law school. Don't assume public schools will be the best deal. After all, out-of-state tuition can be astronomical, and the better scholarships might come from private universities because they can be more flexible in what they offer to you (particularly as an out-of-state applicant).

I often see that at the beginning of the cycle, people are really focused on getting into the best-ranked school, but as they get closer to signing on the dotted line, their priorities change, and they wish they had more scholarships to choose from and find themselves lured by a school that wouldn't have tempted them a few months earlier.

If you are looking for scholarships, it's going to be based primarily on your numbers. Once you have your LSAT and GPA, look for schools where your numbers place you above the median, and near the 75th percentile, of admitted students. You can find this information on school websites or search for schools using the LSAC Admission Calculator.

For people willing to go almost anywhere in the country, who are less concerned with the cost of law school, here is how I suggest picking schools to apply to: first, cast a wide net. There is no magic number of schools to apply to for one simple reason—it does no good for me to tell you to apply to fifteen law schools if ten of them are schools you have no hope of getting into. It's important to put schools into categories. Pick some schools where they take 15 percent or fewer of people with your numbers. These are your reach schools. (A school that never takes anyone with your numbers is not a reach school—it's a waste of an application; no, people don't get into Harvard Law by accident.) If you have good soft factors, you should keep your options open by going heavy on the reach schools. They can even be more than half of your total applications.

Most of your schools list should be midrange schools. That means that your numbers fall between the 25th and 75th percentiles for those schools. Some people within this range are admitted and some aren't. This is where your brilliant personal statement, optional essays, résumé, LORs, and soft factors come in to play.

It's always good to pick two to four safety schools. However, if you have problems in your application like an arrest or two, some other character and fitness issue of significance, or some other weakness (like a downward trend with grades or an unimpressive résumé), then you need to go heavy on the safety schools, and this should be the bulk of your application list.

Except for the person who knows that moving is not a possibility, I like my clients to keep their options open. Over thirteen years as a law school admission consultant, I have seen people change their minds dramatically over the six to nine months between when they are deciding where to apply and when they have to choose where to attend. At first, people tend to think rankings are most important. And even if someone sticks to this philosophy, when the new rankings are released (right before deposit deadlines), the order of preference can change (which is pretty lame, if you ask me). Law schools don't change significantly from year to year, but U.S. News has to change the rankings, or no one would buy their magazine or blog or tweet about the rankings.

I see that scholarships become more important to people as they get closer to actually taking out loans in the amount of a mortgage. Also, people might enter into serious relationships or have family issues arise that make a certain location especially appealing. This is why I think all applicants should apply to schools that (1) are near a place they consider home, (2) are in a place where they would be happy living their lives and pursuing their careers, (3) are reasonably priced, and (4) would be their dream to attend. If you cover all of these bases while balancing your reach/midrange/safety positioning, you should end up with an array of good choices to make no matter where life might take you between the time you apply and the time when you have to commit to a school.

For those of you thinking that none of this applies to you because you only want to go to law school if you can get into Yale, Harvard, or Stanford, my first question is, "do you really want to go to law school, or do you want a brand name on your sweatshirt?" My second question is, "do you have what it takes?" It amazes me how many calls I get from people with mediocre credentials who feel they are special, and they will be the person Harvard takes with a 148 and a 3.2. (It's not going to happen unless you can take credit for stopping civil war in Syria). If you have an LSAT score in the mid-170s and a 3.9 GPA from a very good school, you've written a thesis, run a nonprofit (or for-profit for that matter), and have a lot of great stuff going for you, then you're a great candidate for Harvard, Yale, and Stanford. You could just apply to these three, but most people in this category are humble enough to think they need to apply to at least the top five or six law schools. I had a client this year who fell into this category—a 177, a 3.9 from a strong undergraduate school, and an interesting résumé. I told her she only needed to apply to the top three, but because scholarships should be part of her consideration, she should apply to a few top ten schools as well. It's always good to have options, and of course she received fee waivers to schools based on her credentials.

If you are open to different locations, your schools list will inevitably grow as you progress through the cycle because schools will throw application fee waivers at your feet. You will get an e-mail from Cornell or some other dream school offering you a free application and you will think, "Me! They want ME!" But they don't necessarily. In addition to wanting the best students, they want to keep their application numbers high, so that they can keep their acceptance rates low. If you were planning to apply to that school anyway, please go ahead and do so. But consider making sure they know you were going to apply anyway and that you have a high level of interest so that they don't put you in the waiting list pile because they assume you only applied because of the fee waiver.

You can, and should, visit schools when it is convenient and affordable for you to do so. The more you sit in on classes at law schools and talk with students at different schools, the better idea you'll get of what a school is really like and whether you can see yourself there. Visiting a law school while you're in the application process also shows interest and gives you something specific to say about reasons for your interest in a school (if the personal statement or optional essays give you that opportunity).

Key Takeaways

- Apply to schools that are reaches and dreams, but where students with your numbers are accepted each year.
- Cast a wider net with applications if you'd like to consider scholarship offers.
- Avoid getting too attached to the U.S. News Rankings; they do change each year. Look at other ways of ranking schools, including Law School Transparency's online tools (including LSTPro) and Above The Law's annual ranking of the top fifty law schools.
- Make time to visit law schools.

CHAPTER 12

PREPARING FOR INTERVIEWS

Will I Have to Interview with Law Schools?

Most law schools do not interview applicants. There are simply too many applicants to handle this. However, interviews are becoming more commonplace. There are four kinds of "interviews" in the law school admission process:

1. Informal: You make an appointment with the admission office, and you do not call it an interview but you do get (very often) one-on-one face time with someone who is a decision maker. From your end, the purpose is to become more than just a paper application so that they can put a face to the name and you can make a favorable impression, address any perceived weaknesses, express your interest in the school, and gain advice about how to move forward.

2. Strongly Suggested: Northwestern and Vanderbilt strongly suggest applicants sign up for an interview, either on campus or with an alumna in your hometown. One of my clients said this about her experience: "I met with an alum (who seemed to be in his mid to late sixties), and he pretty much just asked me what my interest in Vanderbilt was and then asked me specific questions that he had from looking at my résumé." (She was admitted with a high 150s LSAT score). My clients who interview on campus with someone in the admissions office at Northwestern find it

very straightforward. The interviewer has seen the applicant's résumé and asks about the experiences on it.

3. Requested: Harvard has been interviewing people via Skype by invitation only, as have the Universities of Chicago and Columbia, for example. This is really a check to make sure you're not a crazy person, that you are who you say you are, and that you have some social skills. One of my clients told me that this interview felt a bit like she was being grilled on her academic background and that the twenty-minute time frame was strictly adhered to. She was pretty worried about how it went, but in the end, she was admitted. Another client was questioned about why she wanted to go to law school instead of business school. One of my clients who had Skype interviews at both Chicago and Georgetown said he quickly realized the interviewer was not there to trick him but instead genuinely wanted to know him better. It's interesting that a current law student at the University of Chicago told me that a professor remarked that the quality of students has improved since the school began interviewing applicants before admitting them, and I believe it! Schools are using technology and a smaller applicant pool to pick personable, interesting people.

Georgetown has also been holding group interviews by invitation. For example, one of my clients attended a group interview in the Bay Area for applicants from Berkeley and Stanford. This was a completely different ball game: the participants were given two examples of law school applicants and asked whom to admit! It was a test of the ability to think on your feet, to lead without being dominating, and to support your stance. Just showing up gives you the opportunity to show interest in attending. (Georgetown doesn't invite all applicants to do this; some applicants are never asked for an interview; others get alumni interviews).

A number of schools have been doing brief phone interviews prior to accepting applicants in some cases, including University of Virginia, University of California, Los Angeles, and Washington University St. Louis.

4. Recorded Video Interviews: I hate these. They are horrible. (I'm looking at you, Cornell, Northwestern, and Seton Hall.) They give you a chance to record yourself under timed conditions, and some of them even tack on a written response.

Sample Interview Questions to Help You Prepare:

- Why this law school?
- Why law?
- What career would you choose if you could not practice law?
- Identify a strength and a weakness.
- Discuss a time when you worked as part of a team.
- Tell me about a time when you solved a problem.
- What is the most influential book you've read?
- Should we have compulsory voting?
- If you could advise the president on any policy issue, what would it be and what would you say?
- Why did you choose to work for X?
- What is your favorite class you took in college?
- What are your five and ten year goals?

Scholarship Interviews

There are schools that incorporate interviews as part of the process to receive certain scholarships, including NYU, Duke, Chicago, and even Southwestern. Some of these are in person, and some are via Skype. Duke has been interviewing admitted students to gauge their interest and the amount of financial assistance they would need in order to seriously consider attending. Some select scholarships involve interviews; usually these are public-interest scholarships. One of my clients interviewed for a scholarship at the University of Pennsylvania School of Law, and the panel included four people, including two practicing public-interest lawyers. They asked about her interest in the program and her goals, and they inquired more specifically into the area of public-interest law that she hoped to practice. Part of her expenses for travel to the interview were covered by the school.

Tips:

- Remember to test Skype before the interview. Check the lighting and what is in view of your camera.
- Have someone do a mock interview with you—practice how you would answer questions.
- Dress professionally.
- Remove anything distracting from behind you or around you.
- Avoid looking at notes or sounding rehearsed. (There is a fine line between being prepared and sounding rehearsed).
- Have two to three questions ready about the school that show you've done your research and that you can envision yourself as a student there. Avoid anything obviously stated on the website or asking, "When will I hear from you?" and "What are my chances of admission" questions.
- Sound competent, interesting, thoughtful, authentic, appropriate, and not needy.

Key Takeaways

- Research whether the law schools on your list encourage interviews.
- When asked to interview, take time to prepare your responses to questions including "Why law school?" and "Why our law school?"
- Follow up with thank-you notes to interviewers, reiterating your interest in the school.

CHAPTER 13

FILLING OUT APPLICATIONS

What Do I Need to Decide before Filling Out Applications?

First, will you be applying under an Early Decision Program? If so, be sure to select that application on LSAC. Second, consider whether you will you be applying full-time or part-time.

Here are some things to consider regarding part time programs:

- If you have not been in school for a long time, haven't been the world's best student, and/or you would like to continue working during your first year of law school, then consider applying part-time to law schools that offer this as an option. You will take one fewer class each semester, and if you make up the two classes during the summer after your first year, you can usually transfer into the full-time program and graduate in three years. Otherwise, you are not permitted to work during your first year of law school. You are permitted to work up to twenty hours per week as a 2L and 3L, or full-time if you attend law school only part-time. There are ABA rules regulating these things, and if you are curious about work restrictions and related issues, you should look into these rules (www.americanbar.org/content/dam/aba/migrated/legaled/standards/20072008standardsWeb Content/Chapter_3.authcheckdam.pdf).
- It is not possible to "dabble" in law school—you will not be able to take one or two classes at a time until you finally graduate. The

ABA requires that you finish your degree no later than eighty-four months after starting law school (ABA Standard 304(c)). This can't be reset by transferring schools.

- If you begin law school part-time and then want to transfer to another law school, you will most likely be restricted to transferring to another part-time program because you will not have earned a sufficient number of credits to be compared with other 1Ls and/or to begin your second year of law school.

- Do you want to have a social life? If you would be happiest surrounded by students who may be older, working, married, with families and/or with professional careers under their belts, then you would probably be very comfortable in a part-time program. If, however, you will deeply regret the sounds of joy coming from the Quad during Thursday night keg parties sponsored by the Student Bar Association while you are stuck in Contracts or Torts, then attending school at night probably isn't a good idea.

- Some law schools offer year-round two-year JD programs. One of my former clients who was ten years out of college decided to do Southwestern Law School's SCALE program and saved $40,000.

- If you are an international student, you are not going to be able to attend law school part-time under your visa restrictions.

What Should I Know before Filling Out Applications?

First, the process is all online through LSAC. Thank God. (This wasn't always the case). What you enter for one application is (mostly) automatically completed in subsequent applications. But there are still a lot of opportunities for mistakes.

Here are things to keep in mind:

1. Make sure to fill out every question that is required.
2. Make sure your responses fit in the space provided. Sometimes things are cut off rather awkwardly.
3. Check punctuation and capitalization.
4. Do not check too many areas of interest of law—selecting more than three or four is overkill. And don't say you are interested in

something just because you think a school is known for it. Make sure your stated area(s) of interest are consistent with other areas of your application.

5. Attach the correct documents.

6. Do not attach anything extra with your application such as copies of your thesis or newspaper articles where you are featured. No certificates of achievement or pictures of yourself with President Obama. (Ah, the good old days...)

7. Be sure that tracked changes aren't showing up on your attached documents because LSAC turns your Word documents into PDFs for you when you attach them.

8. Check each school's website and application instructions to be sure you are submitting exactly what the law school is looking for.

9. Make sure employment dates are consistent between your application and your résumé.

10. Make sure your formatting is consistent between all attachments: usually this means double spacing with a serif-font, 11 or 12 point in size, with one inch margins and a header on each page that includes your name, LSAC ID#, the document heading ("Personal Statement" or "Addendum"), and the page number.

11. Avoid typos. Do everything within your power to make sure they don't happen. If they do happen, and you catch one after the application is submitted, do everything within your power not to throw yourself on the bed and cry or jump off a bridge. For example, I wanted to ugly cry after finding errors in the last edition of this book. I tried to make it sound purposeful when someone called me out on Twitter for having a typo in the "no typos" paragraph. When you contact me to let me know about mistakes in this edition of the book, I will practice my French: *c'est la vie*. I know the book will still be a bestseller and still be valuable to law school applicants, and one mistake won't detract from that. The same is true with your application. However, a mistake-riddled application diminishes your credibility with the law school, so take the extra time and take care.

12. Don't send School A's personal statement to School B. Nothing you can do about that one once it's done. You can't just ask the school to replace your essay in the PDF file that is your application. You're stuck. You can apologize, but it's really lame and embarrassing.

13. Print out each application and check it before submitting it. Ask someone else to check it also.

14. Avoid submitting things late at night. This is when mistakes happen. If you're exhausted, wait until the next day to submit the application. You only get one shot; make sure it's perfect. (When I first wrote this book, I think I referred to an Eminem song on this line, but now I think readers will better relate to the line in the soundtrack of *Hamilton*.) Remember, except in extreme circumstances, waiting a day won't make a difference, but a mistake in your application could make all the difference.

After Submitting Applications

- Consider visiting schools that are easily accessible to you geographically. Most law schools will allow you to arrange these visits through the admission office, go on a tour of the law school, sit in on a class, and even meet with an admission counselor.

- Avoid reading the message boards, particularly on Top-law-schools.com. One of my clients, who got into Georgetown Law with a 160 LSAT, said, "My girlfriend took everything on there like it was written in the Bible. If someone cares that much to write about how bad certain schools are, they probably should be spending their time doing something else more constructive. My girlfriend would drive herself insane seeing people post that they would get a call or they would get accepted, and she hadn't heard anything yet. She was a wreck when she heard someone got an interview at G'town and then two days later they called her in. I didn't even get an interview and got in. My advice: be like a race-horse; put on your blinders and run your race. Don't stress about what other people are getting or doing, just focus on your apps."

- If you're between two or three schools and can't decide, I highly recommend going to the admitted student open houses or visiting at a time that is more convenient for you. "It can be really eye-opening: you may hate one place that you were sold on and fall in love with a place you weren't considering strongly," said a third-year law student.

Key Takeaways

- Consider whether a Binding Early Decision agreement is right for you.
- Consider whether to apply part-time or full-time.
- Eliminate all errors in applications; check everything at least twice.

CHAPTER 14

PURSUING A WAITING LIST

What Do I Do Now That I am on a Waiting List?

Don't despair: on a waiting list, you are still in the running. On a waiting list, you still have some control over your future. On a waiting list, you can get into your dream law school. That's why I say "Congratulations!" A waiting list means hope! (As does a "held" and "reserve" decision, by the way). Many law schools end up enrolling a significant portion of their class from the waiting list.

However, you will need to send a deposit to a school you've already been admitted to while you get busy waiting. Most law schools don't even think about the people on their waiting list until after they have the first deposits from the people they've admitted. Only once they see how those numbers come back (and how many seats may still be available in their class and how much they are committed to in terms of scholarships) do they start to evaluate their wait-listed applicants.

When a law school starts to review a waiting list to admit people, they may have specific needs. For example, if more women sent deposits than men, they may need to balance out the class by looking for men from the waiting-list pool. If the LSAT numbers for the entering class are looking strong, but the GPAs are looking low, they may go to people with strong GPAs. They might see that they have too many people from a certain undergrad school and not enough from another or by geographic region or there is room to expand upon ethnic diversity. These are all considerations when deciding who will be admitted. And, the number one thing they are looking for within these categories is finding the person who is most likely to attend after being offered a seat.

This is why showing interest is important and not just submitting the form accepting your place on the waiting list. When a spot opens up, the dean of admissions is thinking, "Who do I like? Whose day do I want to make?" After all, this is one of the most fun things an admission officer gets to do. I want to call someone who I know is going to be very happy to hear from me. I get to be a hero today! So who do I call? That nice kid who has been in touch with me for six months! The guy who works down the street as a paralegal! The young woman who traveled from Ohio to visit the law school! This is where making effort makes all the difference. After all, I don't want to have to make five calls to get someone who is happy to hear from me. I want the person who is the sure thing because what I don't want is to admit someone at this point in the year who is not going to attend.

If you do absolutely nothing beyond accepting your place on the waiting list, you will not get into the law school. That's all there is to it. You must go above and beyond. You must launch your campaign to get in. If this chapter is more pep talk than tips, it's because I've seen too many people discouraged by a waiting-list decision when they should be encouraged by it. People give up too soon. Also, people assume there will be no scholarship offers from schools where they are admitted off the waiting list. This used to be the case, but in recent years, this has changed and more schools are reserving (or redistributing) scholarship funds after deposit deadlines to both admitted students and those who are newly admitted from the waiting list.

Most waiting-list movement comes in May, June, and July. Of course, I've had clients receive calls from their top choice law school while sitting in Orientation at their second-choice law school. Sometimes this happens, and it can be an awesome (if stressful) thing. But most waiting-list news comes in plenty of time for you to enter into a lease and buy books. Keep yourself in the running if it's a school you would choose over the one where you are currently holding a seat.

Here is a schedule of things you can do when you find out you are wait-listed:

1. Immediately and enthusiastically accept a place on the waiting list. Refrain from immediately bombarding the law school with

letters and additional information, especially if you get your waiting-list notification before March.

2. Schedule a campus tour and visit if you have not already done so and if it is economically feasible for you to do so. If you live in the same city or state and haven't visited, the school isn't going to think you're very interested in attending. Does this really help? People ask me that all the time. I had a client who was absolutely dying to go to law school, and he didn't care where so long as he could practice law one day. He flew himself across the country to visit a law school where he was wait-listed, where he'd been told he would have ten minutes with the assistant director of admissions. The ten minutes turned into an hour, and two days later he was admitted.

3. During your visit, try to get some face time (don't ask for an "interview") with an admission counselor. Ask about the waiting list and what they recommend in terms of keeping in touch and then follow that to the letter. Talk to everyone you meet—ask students about their experiences at the law school, ask them what they did if they were wait-listed, introduce yourself to the professor whose class you are visiting, and follow up by writing thank-you notes (by e-mail) to each of them.

4. Immediately after the deposit deadlines (since there is sometimes more than one), follow up with a letter expressing your interest in attending the law school—be specific! Beware of using sample Letters of Continued Interest—I see the same language repeated in initial drafts done by my clients, and I know the law schools see it too. It's very obvious when you've copied a form or sample. Speak from the heart, and get your message across. There's no reason to use the awkward and unnatural phrase "continuing interest" in this letter.

5. As you receive new (superb) grades and/or honors and/or promotions at work, or take on a new job or leadership position, e-mail the admissions office with the news. If you plan to travel out of the country and need to be reached in a different way, let them know that as well.

6. Refrain from stalking the admissions office. Keep in touch every month until deposit deadlines have passed, then maybe every two to four weeks depending on the vibe you are getting from the school's communications with you and whether you have real updates to pass along.

7. If you feel very confident in your ability to raise your LSAT score by more than two points, then consider a June retake. You would probably still be on the waiting list in June and improving your LSAT score could make the difference.

8. Some law schools specifically invite you to submit additional essays. If you pass this opportunity by, the law school will assume you are not interested in attending. For example, the University of Texas often asks people to supplement their applications after the fact with reasons for their interest in the school. If you don't do it, you won't be admitted.

Some waiting-list success stories:

- "I was wait-listed at Loyola New Orleans College of Law. I set a meeting with the dean of admissions, drove from Tallahassee to New Orleans, and argued my first case as a would-be lawyer (my admission). I received my letter of admission in June and went on to graduate cum laude."

- "I got off the BU waiting list in mid-May. The Fordham waiting list came a few weeks after that. The things I did for Fordham included meeting with a professor with whom I had a connection (he then made a call to the admissions office on my behalf) and then at that point they offered me a spot in the evening program. After that, I called the admissions office and explained to them that I only wanted to attend full-time, that I had already gotten off the waiting list at BU, and that I would go there if Fordham didn't have a spot. That person called me back within ten minutes to offer me a place in the full-time program. It can be done! Being a self-advocate can be incredibly daunting, but it was a great lesson for me in how to be an advocate before I even got to law school."

- "I was notified that I had been placed on the waiting list in February. Around the middle of March, BC e-mailed me asking if I was still interested in remaining on the waiting list. I immediately replied that BC was one of my top choices, and I would be happy to submit any additional materials if need be. I didn't do anything but wait, and by the end of the month BC Law Admissions notified me that I had been accepted!"

- "I found out I was wait-listed, so I decided to visit the law school to see if I wanted to continue campaigning to get in. On Fridays, the school does these Q&A sessions with some people from admissions, and the person doing it that week happened to be the dean of admissions. Luckily for me, there were only three of us visiting that day, so she offered to meet with us one on one. We had a really great conversation, and she called me the next day offering me a spot. It was such a great feeling, and I'm so glad I took the time to visit!"

- "I followed Ann's advice and sent a letter every month and then every three weeks as it got closer. I visited most of the schools, and sent them various e-mails that I had been engaged in various activities in school and that my grades were improving. I got into GULC!"

- "I was wait-listed by two schools during the last application cycle. I was very upset about it at the time, but I took action to turn my spots on the waiting lists into acceptances. I initially sent letters of continued interest. I made sure to stress to my top choice school that I would attend and withdraw all other applications if admitted. I also sent e-mails to both schools expressing my interest about every three weeks during the school year and every two weeks during the summer. For, example, I e-mailed them about updating my résumé since I was interning at a law firm and got a job for the summer. I got into one of the schools in early June and the other one around mid-July. I had sent in an e-mail to the second school just the day before I got accepted, so I definitely think sending the admissions office e-mails and reminding them how much you care can really make a difference to have them keep you in mind!"

- "I was wait-listed at Penn in March. Immediately upon receiving my placement on the waiting list, Ann instructed me to go straight to the school, visit the campus, visit admissions, and meet with anyone to get more information of not only the process but also about the school itself. I visited that week and spoke to the receptionist at the Admissions Office of Penn. I told her that Penn was the place for me, but that hopefully, I would be the person for Penn. After my visit, I wrote a Letter of Continued Interest, specifically thanking her for the information she gave me. When I received my call for admission in early May, the director of admissions told me that the receptionist had immediately noted my interest in Penn and passed the word around the office. Being present and being active in the admission process was a major factor in my admission to Penn even after having been wait-listed." (**Note from Ann:** I think it was also important that he was nice *to the receptionist.* Remember that the person who answers the phone and sits behind the desk is the gatekeeper, and treating that person unprofessionally can harpoon your chances of admission.)
- "I got into my top choice school, NYU, off the waiting list while I was participating in orientation at another law school. I knew NYU was a far reach, but I kept in touch with the admissions office through the spring and summer by sending letters of continued interest. When the admissions office e-mailed me in mid-August to ask if I wanted to stay on the waiting list, I reiterated my interest. The rest is history."

Key Takeways

- A waiting-list decision means you're still in the running.
- Launch a protracted campaign to turn that decision into an acceptance.
- Prepare yourself for a marathon, not a sprint.
- You will need to send a seat deposit to a school where you've been admitted and just risk losing the deposit if you decide to attend elsewhere.

CHAPTER 15

CHOOSING YOUR LAW SCHOOL

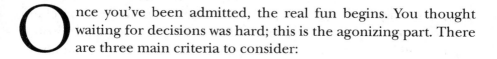nce you've been admitted, the real fun begins. You thought waiting for decisions was hard; this is the agonizing part. There are three main criteria to consider:

1. REPUTATION
2. LOCATION
3. COST

The order of importance of these three factors varies based on what is most important to you. I wrote an entire book about what lawyers think is important in choosing a law school, so if you are at this phase of the process, it's time to read *The Law School Decision Game*.

In this chapter, in the very first version of this book, I wrote the following: "What's Important in a Law School? JOBS. It's that simple. You must consider which school will give you the most access to jobs." This remains true today. There are two ways to choose a law school around jobs—you can go for the jobs that care about the brand name of the school you attend, or you can choose a law school located in the city where you hope to build your law career.

Remember that most law school graduates aren't working in glamorous international law, jet-setting, foreign-policy careers. There is a lot of glamour, I think, in being a criminal defense attorney whose office resembles a shoebox and whose suit is ten years old. (They are certainly more likeable and interesting in how they are portrayed in the movies when going up against the BigLaw lawyers, aren't they?) But these two attorneys may or may not have gone to different law schools. Maybe they both went to Harvard, or maybe one went to Western New England School of Law. The bread and butter of the legal profession didn't need to go to Harvard to do their jobs. But the upper echelon elite positions are not easily accessible to graduates of lower-ranked law schools.

I like to be polite and call them "regional" law schools because most of them are perfectly wonderful places to go if you plan to be a personal injury, civil rights, criminal defense, insurance defense, family law, or trusts and estates attorney. These are the attorneys people and companies need for their everyday problems. This is real roll-up-your-sleeves law. But it's not what most people have visions of doing when they are taking the LSAT. Going to a lower-ranked school will preclude you from clerking on the Supreme Court and becoming a law professor, absolutely, but if you are at the top of your class at a top one hundred school, you will probably still have access to clerkships and BigLaw positions.

In *The Law School Decision Game*, I interviewed nearly three hundred lawyers about their law school decisions, their careers, and the money they make. At the risk of being repetitive, I am going to repeat the main points here because I fear too many of you will be overly idealistic and refuse to read that book, just hoping/wishing/praying everything will work out for you.

Law practice is demanding. The hours are long. And you'll be doing well just by making $100,000 a year, and that's after many years of hard work. I also reached out to some of my former clients for their advice on this subject:

- "Either go to the best school you get into or the school that gives you a full ride. Having Columbia Law on my résumé helped me more with my job search than I could have imagined. On the other hand, if I had no debt I probably wouldn't have been as stressed" (EK, Columbia Law graduate).
- "Frankly, with the current economy and job prospects for law grads, my advice to people has been "Go T-14 or Go for free." If you go that path, you are much more likely to either (a) have a job at graduation or (b) not have debt at graduation. I'm not

sure right now that I would pick Fordham over the option to attend Brooklyn for free. Clearly, Fordham was the best place for me (with strong IP and eight blocks from my apartment), but I am a unicorn who got an in-house job in IP, which is basically unheard of. I think "T-14 or free" really applies to those who don't necessarily know what kind of law they want to practice—a school with specific strengths/alumni networks won't necessarily help someone who doesn't realize until 3L what practice areas excite them" (Sara Yood, Fordham Law graduate).

- "My advice on choosing a law school would be to balance job prospects with debt level. I think limiting debt is incredibly important. Even if you get BigLaw, going to law school at full cost can mean debt hanging over your head for years (and limiting what you are able to do in life). If you don't want BigLaw (and excluding career paths like academia), then I think it only makes sense to try and limit debt as much as possible, unless you want to do public interest and you can go to a school with a good LRAP (Loan Repayment Assistance Program) and good public-interest connections. Also, it's vital to make sure the school you are considering can actually give you a decent shot at a legal job. The sad thing is, especially in this economy, there are a ton of law schools that might just waste three years of your life and leave you only in a worse position than when you started law school" (Brian Bah, University of Texas School of Law graduate).

- Even lower-ranked schools can have great alumni networks. "I recognized that real-world experience and training was highly important because I knew prior to law school that I wanted to be a litigator. I chose Southwestern Law School because it had a trial-focused curriculum and an honors program in trial advocacy. The trial experience I obtained during law school made me a prime candidate for a postgraduate fellowship with the Los Angeles Chapter of the American Board of Trial Advocates, and this fellowship placed me in firms and allowed me to meet seasoned attorneys and some of the best litigators in the country. The alumni network was very interested in hiring the school's graduates. Ultimately, I got my current position because an alumnus of my law school from my fellowship referred me to a colleague in need of a new associate" (Ashlee Clark, Southwestern Law School and trial attorney).

This is another time when discussion forums can be an easy resource but a destructive force in your decision-making. One of my really savvy former clients (now a graduate of NYU Law School), who has spent a lot more time than I have on the Top Law Schools forum, has the following take on it: "Posters with five-digit post counts create elaborate models to determine which schools are better than other schools and people repeat their conclusions as gospel even though they have absolutely no clue where the models or data sets come from or what the potential weaknesses could be. Yes, Virginia is a better bet than George Washington for almost everything, and Carolina will always beat Campbell, but a slavish devotion to conventional wisdom obscures certain things that make certain schools look stronger or weaker than others when they actually aren't...TLS still talks dozens of snow-hating 'Empire State of Mind' or 'California Dreamin'' admits into moving to Ithaca, Ann Arbor, or Chicago every year. It's sad."

Things to Consider

1. Avoid blindly following the rankings. This year's number twenty-one and number seventeen could reverse next year, and then you'd feel dumb for choosing one because it was top twenty. By the time you graduate from law school, either school could be a top fourteen or a top thirty. See my chart below, demonstrating how rankings of the top schools have changed since the time I published the first edition of this book (2009), then the second edition (2013), and today (2017).
2. Talk to graduates of the schools you're considering.
3. Think about the kind of career you envision for yourself and whether the school can get you there. For most legal jobs, any reputable school will train you. Most lawyers aren't negotiating international treaties—they are representing people, insurance companies, and entities. And they graduate from all kinds of law schools.

4. Spend time researching the school through the ABA 509 reports and through Law School Transparency.

Be true to yourself. Don't choose a school because other people will be impressed by it or because people know the school's football program. This is a decision you'll have to live with, so make a choice that feels right to you. If you are not happy with any of your choices, consider reapplying to law school and including different schools, improving your credentials and/or materials, and trying again. Don't make a good-enough short-term decision at the expense of a much better long-term decision. (This mostly applies to people who apply hurriedly, without much preparation, and late in the cycle, who feel they are in a rush to start law school). Remember that this isn't about what your parents want for you—it's about making a decision for your own life.

Don't count on being able to transfer after your first year. Assume when you start at a law school that this is the law school you will graduate from. If you end up excelling during your first year (top 20 percent or above), then you can think about transferring to a different law school. But remember that this isn't so easy when everyone is bright and everyone is motivated and everyone is vying for the same goal of being at the top of the class. Also remember that to make a big jump up in the rankings, you'll have to be even higher in your class. I usually say that you should choose a law school you'd be happy graduating from and that transferring should be something that comes as a nice surprise after you get your first semester's grades. Once you get those great grades, then there are great opportunities to work your way up the rankings. "I met at least six 2L transfers to Harvard Law School this year (from UChicago, NYU and UT), and all of them were unsuccessful applicants the year prior," said a Harvard Law student.

Watch out for the for-profit law schools. (One of my former clients calls them "soul-sucking for-profit scam-schools"). These are often the schools with high rates of 1Ls who don't make it through the first year. Schools that take a lot of people with low numbers are giving them a chance to succeed, but these applicants don't always make it. Sometimes low numbers really do show a person's potential for succeeding in law school. Some of these law schools are actually closing, leaving their students in a bind.

If you're looking at job statistics, don't just look at the self-reported employment number and call it a day: look into whether graduates are in jobs that require JDs, whether the law school is hiring its own graduates to boost the numbers, and check out www.lawschooltransparency.com, a site that should be on every law school applicant's bookmarks.

Consider what salary you expect to make in the first few years out of law school and whether the loans will have been worthwhile. Also consider that some law schools offer LRAPs for people who enter public-interest careers or who take jobs on the lower end of the pay scale. Look into eligibility for these programs at the schools you are considering.

Sending Deposits

It's very common that a school will have an April 1 or April 15 or May 1 deposit deadline, particularly for scholarship recipients, and that you may still be waiting for decisions from some schools at that point. You will likely also be on waiting lists that won't start to move until after the deposit deadlines. You will need to send a deposit to secure your spot. If you end up getting into another school that you would prefer to attend, you simply lose your deposit. No biggie.

You can ask schools to extend these deadlines for a couple of weeks if you haven't yet had time to visit or if you are still waiting for a particular school's decision. As long as you ask nicely, the worst they can say is, "Sorry, no."

You may send deposits to more than one school with the caveat that the schools will know you have sent multiple deposits as of a date (May 15, currently) when schools get an "overlap report." At that point, they can make you put up or shut up, so you'll have to withdraw from one of those schools (hence spots opening up for additional wait-listed candidates at that time). "LSAC provides participating law schools with periodic reports detailing the number of applicants who have submitted seat deposits or commitments at other participating schools, along with identification of those other schools. These reports now include the names and LSAC account numbers for all candidates who have deposits/commitments at multiple participating schools" (see http://www.lsac.org/jd/applying-to-law-school/whom-to-admit/seat-deposits).

Ranking Trends

Here is a chart of the top twenty-five schools (according to U.S. News and World Report, which today is just a rankings machine and not a real news source). The chart shows the rankings during each year that I published an edition of this book. Note that Berkeley slides down over time, and George Washington University makes an appearance in 2014 and then falls off this list (Rankings are labeled for the coming year, not the year in which they are published).

Ranking	2010	2014	2018
1	Yale University	Yale University	Yale University
2	Harvard University	Harvard University (tie for 2)	Stanford University
3	Stanford University	Stanford University (tie for 2)	Harvard University
4	Columbia University	University of Chicago (tie for 4)	University of Chicago
5	New York University	Columbia University (tie for 4)	Columbia University

6	University of California, Berkeley (tie for 6)	New York University	New York University
7	University of Chicago (tie for 6)	University of Pennsylvania (tie for 7)	University of Pennsylvania
8	University of Pennsylvania	University of Virginia (tie for 7)	University of Michigan, Ann Arbor (tie for 8)
9	University of Michigan, Ann Arbor	University of California, Berkeley (tie for 9)	University of Virginia (tie for 8)
10	Duke University (tie for 10)	University of Michigan, Ann Arbor (tie for 9)	Duke University (tie for 10)

11	Northwestern University (tie for 10)	Duke University	Northwestern University (tie for 10)
12	University of Virginia (tie for 10)	Northwestern University	University of California, Berkeley
13	Cornell University	Cornell University	Cornell University
14	Georgetown University	Georgetown University	University of Texas, Austin
15	University of California, Los Angeles (tie for 15)	University of Texas, Austin (tie for 15)	Georgetown University (tie for 15)

16	University of Texas, Austin (tie for 15)	Vanderbilt University (tie for 15)	University of California, Los Angeles (tie for 15)
17	Vanderbilt University	University of California, Los Angeles	Vanderbilt University
18	University of Southern California	University of Southern California	Washington University in St. Louis
19	Washington University in St. Louis	University of Minnesota, Twin Cities (tie for 19)	University of Southern California
20	Boston University (tie for 20)	Washington University in St. Louis (tie for 19)	University of Iowa (tie for 20)

21	Emory University (tie for 20)	George Washington University (tie for 21)	University of Notre Dame (tie for 20)
22	University of Minnesota (tie for 20)	University of Alabama (tie for 21)	Emory University
23	University of Indiana, Bloomington (tie for 23)	Emory University (tie for 23)	Boston University (tie for 23)
24	University of Illinois (tie for 23)	University of Notre Dame (tie for 23)	University of Minnesota (tie for 23)
25	University of Notre Dame (tie for 23)	Indiana University, Bloomington	Arizona State University

Selected Schools	2010	2014	2018
Alabama	30 (tie)	21 (tie)	26th (tie)
Irvine	unranked	unranked	28 (tie)
Washington and Lee	30 (tie)	43 (tie)	28 (tie)
Miami	71 (tie)	61 (tie)	77 (tie)

Is Washington and Lee really that much better of a school than it was four years ago? Are things just coming back around and averaging out? Alabama looks like a big drop in the last four years, but it's a lift from where it was in 2010. Look at George Washington University—everyone was so excited when it made 25, but now what? It's tied for 30th, but it's still the second-best law school in the DC area, right? Look at trends—if a school has consistently been trending up for ten years, or down for ten years, then that might be cause for concern. A school's reputation ranking may be injured by recent headlines about its dean (see University of Illinois—now ranked 44th—for example, and in a couple years it's all forgotten). Does this really impact who gets clerkships and who gets hired? Try not to fixate on U.S. News. Create criteria of what's important to you and then research the answers to create your own version of rankings.

Key Takeaways

- Remember that the rankings are not a bible.
- You can submit multiple deposits until May 15.
- Consider cost, location, and reputation when deciding where to attend.

CHAPTER 16

TAKE OUR ADVICE

What Should I Know before Going to Law School?

I could (and did!) write a whole book on this subject. See *The Law School Decision Game: A Playbook for Prospective Lawyers*. You need to know that law school is right for you, that you can afford a law degree (now and in the future), and the sacrifices you will be making in the process.

You need to know what to expect from the law school experience.

You need to know what's going to be demanded of you in the classroom and what you should be working on to put on your résumé in terms of activities at the law school.

You need to be ready to network in order to find a job. The best thing you could do right now for yourself (whether you end up going to law school or not) is to learn how to network effectively, how to reach out to people, make contacts, and learn about opportunities as they arise. This is the only way to become a successful professional. Your time starts now.

Academic Performance

Some of my former clients provided advice that is helpful to have before starting law school:

- "As someone who had wanted to go to law school for a long time, the experience I have had thus far was surprising. I didn't excel (despite having a near-perfect undergraduate GPA). I have gotten Bs and a few B- and have had a harder time finding my place than I anticipated. A lot of it has had to do with my attitude and in some part the bad advice I got before going to law school. The worst piece of advice that I got was that you don't learn how to be a lawyer in law school. Having been told this repeatedly, I went into law school with a horrible attitude of thinking, 'These people have nothing to teach me, so why pay attention?' and I really missed a lot of the substantive law I should have absorbed in my first year. During my second year, I really paid attention and—lo and behold—I really know about corporations now, etc. So, to sum up, you do learn law in law school, and it is important. The second worst piece of advice I got was that no matter how hard you try, you won't do well, law school is too hard. What a joke. As with anything in life, usually you get out of it what you put in. If you go into the experience already thinking that no matter how hard you work you won't get results, it really offers little motivation to try hard. The people who I watched bust their butts did really well. End of story. Someone else told me that grades don't matter and that I shouldn't do journal because it is boring. Even if you aren't looking for that BigLaw job, public-interest work is still super competitive, and you need to have the best credentials possible. Unfortunately, the system still values grades and certain checkmarks on the résumé: employers want to see grades and particular activities. And networking during your first year is super important. Some good advice that I received was that you really, really, really shouldn't go to law school until you are ready to put in the work it requires. Law school is the hardest thing I have ever done, and I am not sure even I was ready to take on that commitment" (EK, a graduate of Columbia Law School).

- "Choose classes for 2L and 3L year wisely. Look at teacher evaluations, look to see if they have past exams and if those are in a format that you are good at, look at past grade distributions for that professor, talk to other law students about the class and the professor. Most importantly, make sure you are interested in the content. Don't take Wills and Estates just because everyone else is doing it or because it's on the bar if you think you will be bored to death in the class. It's important not to fall into groupthink. There is not one perfect way to study—you need to find out what works best for you, even if that's different from what others are doing. You need to think long and hard about what you want your legal career to be and talk to professors and lawyers actually doing what you want to do to see if your plans are realistic and attainable. This might be based on school, but there can be this magnetic draw to BigLaw and clerkships. If that's what you want to do, that's fine. If you haven't thought about it, then think about it. Don't compete for top stuff just because it's the top stuff. Make sure it's actually stuff you want" (Brian Bah, graduate of the University of Texas School of Law).

- It's impossible to predict how you will do in law school. Being in the middle of a top ten school doesn't necessarily translate to being number one at a school ranked one hundred; there are smart people at every school and other factors than intelligence (like stress management) can impact where you fall in a class" (Rebecca Sivitz, graduate of the University of Pennsylvania School of Law).

- "Making friends with a few professors will take you far after law school. They're great people to get to know because they are the ones with connections in the real world" (Alyssa Tornberg, graduate of Quinnipiac Law).

- "Go to office hours. Start going at the beginning of the semester and try to keep it up throughout. For some classes and some professors it's more helpful than others, but it's a great way to force yourself to dig deep in to the material to look for good questions, and it helps you find professors that you click with. This can be important when it comes to references for jobs and clerkships" (Brian Bah, University of Texas School of Law graduate).

Law Journals

The value of participating on a journal is widely debated, but if you want to work in BigLaw, be a clerk for a judge, and/or enter academia, then you may decide that working on a law review is necessary. Here is a smattering of comments from my former clients regarding their work on law journals—they are all across the board:

- "I do not regret doing law review at all. It can be time consuming, but it's made me so much better at *The Bluebook* and editing in general" (Brian Bah, University of Texas School of Law graduate).
- "Law review/journal isn't worth the one line on your résumé. Almost everyone I know said it took up way too much time for little to nothing in return" (Alyssa Tornberg, Quinnipiac Law graduate).
- "My specialized journal led to a job opportunity which included working on a SCOTUS case. Had I not had the journal, I wouldn't have gotten the job!" (Sara Yood, Fordham Law graduate)
- "In Philly, and in pretty much the entire Delaware Valley, I think being on law review is hugely helpful (at least if you want to work at a firm—it might be a different scenario for public interest or other areas). I know that at my school, those of us with BigLaw internships lined up for the summer are on *Law Review* or another journal. I was actually asked about my case note topic in every interview. It definitely takes a lot of time, but I haven't heard of anyone at my school who regrets participating. Here, law review is 95 percent grade-ons and 5 percent write-ons, which means that in addition to having the journal on your résumé, you're usually highly ranked in the class" (Katie Hester, Villanova Law student).

Law School Advice

- "When I was deciding on whether to clerk, I talked with a professor who said that I should think about it like an apprenticeship. After three years of law school, you get to work closely with an intelligent, experienced mentor. Whether you know precisely what type of law you want to practice or are still figuring that out, you will get excellent practical experience learning about all sorts of areas of law, improving your writing, and honing your debating skills that will help you no matter what your next step is," said a University of Chicago law student.

- "It's important to make friends who are ahead of you in law school. My 2L and 3L friends last year were my saving grace, my shining light, the best thing I had at school. Whether it be a peer mentor or, in my case, all my friends from the softball team, they will be your best source of information, answers to questions, etc. 1Ls are in a 24/7 collective panic. I mean, it's 1L. Everyone is trying to run to attend, do, and compete in anything and everything. Being able to hear what things like exams, professors, moot-court/mock-trial competitions, journal, outlines, etc. are actually like is literal gold. Just from my friendships with softball people I got my best outlines, tutors, help with mock-trial competition, help picking journal, classes 2L & 3L year, and, if nothing else, a much-needed break from 1L. Sometimes you just need to grab a drink with people who aren't stressing about work and grades. Join organizations you want to join, grab coffee or lunch with your peer mentor (they get a budget to do so at G'town), just put yourself out there" (Jon Rausch, Georgetown Law student).

Key Takeaways

- Be prepared to work hard wherever you go.
- Make friends with 2Ls and 3Ls, and lean on them for advice.
- Consider whether a law journal is worthwhile given your career goals.

CHAPTER 17

ADVICE FOR PARENTS OF APPLICANTS

Over the last five years, I've seen an increase in the number of parents reaching out to me who have read my book. As a result, I'm including—for the first time—a chapter with advice and insights for parents of law school applicants. Sometimes the parents call me because they are immigrants and are uninformed about the process of applying to law school in the United States, and they want to give their son or daughter access to a knowledgeable person. Sometimes the parents are lawyers and have an understanding that a lot has changed in the twenty-five years since they applied to law school. These parents often have similar questions despite their different backgrounds. Many of them, such as which law schools are attainable and what will happen if there is an arrest or honor code violation on an applicant's record, are addressed elsewhere in the book. However, I wanted to add a brief note, parent-to-parent, law-school-admission-consultant-to-parent.

I have two daughters in middle school; one is already a teenager. I understand the hopes and dreams we have for our kids. I see the circus of anxiety that can surround the college admission process and how that carries over into my college-aged clients who sometimes pick schools and majors for the wrong reasons, who often face their first struggles—personally and academically—during their college years. As parents, we want our kids to be happy. We want to help them in every way we can to find their version of happy. Sometimes in our "helping" and urging, we fail to understand that our advice and encouragement is perceived as pressure.

The hard part about parenting through this time is letting young people decide for themselves what will make them happy and letting our kids experience failures along the journey as they figure this out. If you're reading this book, you have a child in college or even beyond college, and you know that attending a certain college isn't what makes a person happy—it's the experiences they seek and grow from while they are in college, the gratification they feel at their own accomplishments, especially when achieved in the face of challenges, the way they feel alive when they pursue their passions, and learn from the people around them. Law school is very much the same.

For this reason, I urge you to not make law school another stepping-stone on a prescribed ladder to success. There is not just one way to be successful, just as there is not just one way to be happy. A great read on this topic is *Where You Go Is Not Who You'll Be*, a book I referenced earlier, which describes how the elite schools do not have a lock on Fortune 500 CEOs, Fulbright Scholars and other award winners, or financial success or personal happiness generally. These can be obtained from a wide range of places, as can a successful career in law. Give your (adult) child the gift of being able to explore success and happiness in his or her own way. Offer your support and resources, but try to withhold judgment. It will make the law school admission process less stressful for you both and will be better for your relationship as well.

If you find that you are really the one pulling the weight during this exploratory "getting ready to apply" phase by researching the law school application process, law schools, and LSAT preparation companies, please take a step back. Parents often tell me they are the ones calling me because their child is too busy with school, internships, and so on to do the legwork. I'm happy to talk with parents during a free initial consultation, but after that I insist that the person actually applying to law school steers the ship from there.

Let's be honest, no one is too busy to do what's really important. I promise your kid is binge-watching the newest Amazon series, playing video games, and/or posting on Instagram or Snapchat. He or she can stop to read a blog or listen to a podcast on a commute and to register for the LSAT at midnight after getting home from a social gathering. We find the time for the things that matter. After all, reading this book should take just three or four hours. In my experience, the students who aren't doing the legwork themselves don't stop to think about whether they really want to go to law school at this point in their lives. If they want it, they'll find the time to jump through the hoops. And if they don't want it, they shouldn't be doing it.

The best way you can support your adult child through this process is by advising them about trustworthy resources (such as this book), helping pay for assistance with LSAT preparation and/or admission consulting if you are able, and by asking questions and listening. Some great questions to ask may include the following:

1. What issues/headlines related to law and current events are you most interested in?
2. How would you define a meaningful life?
3. How does law school fit with your goals and interests?
4. Can I help you reach out to any legal professionals so that you can ask them questions and/or shadow them to learn more about what they do?
5. Are there any other careers you're considering, and what might be ways to explore those?
6. Where do you see yourself living?
7. What did you like/not like about your undergraduate school? What's important to you in a law school?
8. How do you plan to pay for law school?

Try to avoid asking all these questions in the same conversation. Rather than overwhelm your son or daughter, take the time to open the lines of communication. Make this a continuing conversation. Avoid giving them deadlines or asking, "Have you talked to Professor Jain about your letter of recommendation yet?" (By the way, if you know the names of your child's professors, it might be a clue that you're a bit too involved in the details of his or her life.) If someone can't manage these tasks unsupervised, then they will not make it through law school anyway.

Please do not accompany your child to visit law schools, especially before they are admitted to that school. It's important that he or she be perceived as independent, as a capable adult. Your presence, even if you stay silent, negates that perception. I also urge you not to call schools—they do have caller ID, and they can put two and two together.

If you have contacts at a certain law school, or colleagues or friends who are graduates of a certain law school that your child is interested in attending, please introduce them to your child and let him or her take it from there. Those individuals can choose to reach out to the law schools to put in a good word for your child in a way they feel is appropriate once the application has been submitted.

Make sure you have an honest discussion with your child early in the process about the amount of financial support you'll be able to lend during law school. I've seen many clients who anticipated that their parents would pay for law school who were unpleasantly surprised late in the admission cycle. If you have an honest discussion up front, your son or daughter will know to apply to more schools where scholarship funding is within the realm of possibility and won't suffer the heartbreak of having to say no to a dream school or the overwhelming stress of facing $200,000 in debt for a commitment they already made and cannot undo.

Applying to law school is stressful, and the best role you can play as a parent is as that of the supportive listener. You don't need to read essays or research schools or manage the process. Doing so will not help your family dynamics. Encouraging your child to follow his or her dreams, and to point him or her toward resources, is the right way to go. Let them manage the process from there.

Key Takeaways

- Remember that your "child" is an adult.
- Be supportive but avoid driving the action.
- Ask tough questions to ensure your son or daughter is really considering the options and making good decisions.

APPENDIX

1. Using LSAC: A How-To Guide
2. LSAT Self-Study Schedule

Using LSAC: A How-To Guide
Step 1: Create an LSAC Account

The LSAC is a nonprofit corporation designed to ease the admission process for law schools and their applicants. You can create your LSAC account at lsac.org.

On the home page, select an account type (i.e., **Future JD Student**) from the drop down menu beneath **CREATE NEW ACCOUNT**.

Select **sign up now**.

Input your information, including a username and password that will be used to login in future visits to the site. When complete, hit **Submit**.

You will then be assigned an LSAC Account # that will be displayed on your home page.

Step 2: Obtain an LSAC Fee Waiver (if applicable)

Those with **extreme financial need** may apply for an LSAC Fee Waiver.

From the LSAC home page, select **Apply**.

At the bottom of the page, select **Apply for an LSAC Waiver**.

You will be asked to provide proof of need in the form of tax documentation. LSAC will notify you if you qualify.

Each approved LSAC fee waiver will entitle you to:

- two LSATs (test dates must fall within the two-year waiver period);
- one CAS registration, which includes the Letter of Recommendation Service as well as access to electronic applications for all LSAC-member law schools;
- four CAS Law School Reports (available only after final approval of an LSAC fee waiver); and
- one copy of the *Official LSAT SuperPrep II*™.

Note: Many law schools will waive application fees for those who qualify for the LSAC Fee Waiver.

Step 3: Register with CAS

CAS creates your law school report by combining an academic summary report, LSAT score(s), and writing sample(s), copies of all undergraduate, graduate, and law/professional school transcripts, and LORs. This report will be sent to each law school you apply to.

From the LSAC home page, select **Apply => Credentials**.

You will be required to pay a fee of $175 for the CAS.

You will also be required to pay a fee of $180 to take the Law School Admission Test (LSAT).

Be aware of potential Auxiliary Fees related to the LSAT, such as late registration, test center change, test date change, and hand scoring.

With each application submitted through LSAC, you will be required to pay a $30 fee for CAS to compile a report of your materials to be forwarded to the law school of your choice.

Step 4: Register for the LSAT

You can register for the LSAT from the LSAC home page, select **LSAT => Register for LSAT.**

You will need to provide a photo that will be used on your LSAT admission ticket. You will then see the administration dates and be given your choice of test site locations.

From here, you will also find specific information detailing what will be expected of you on test day.

LSAC will notify you of your LSAT score via e-mail and you can access your detailed results from the LSAC home page by selecting **LSAT => LSAT Status.** If you should need to cancel your LSAT score, you may do that from here as well.

Step 5: Submit Transcripts

Step 6: Submit LORs

From the LSAC home page, select **Apply => Credentials => Letters of Recommendation**.

Here you will find a "How DO I" Guide with detailed instructions on adding recommenders to your account. Be aware that you will need to provide your recommender with a prefilled Letter of Recommendation Form to be submitted with their letter to LSAC. This form can be printed or e-mailed and will assist LSAC in matching your recommender's letter to your account. You will be notified when your letter has been received by LSAC.

It is also on this page that you will be able to assign specific letters to be sent to the law schools of your choice.

Step 7: Register with CRS

CRS will allow you to state various preferences and you will be able to give permission for your information to be shared with law schools. This will allow schools to recruit you based on your specific characteristics and preferences. This tool can be especially useful in acquiring application fee waivers and discovering law schools you may not have considered.

From the LSAC home page, select **My Account => Profile => Candidate Referral Service**.

Step 8: Create a School List

From the LSAC home page, select **Apply**

From this page, select **My School List**

This is where you will be able to search law schools and create a list of schools you would like to apply to. You can access each school's full application from this list.

LSAT Self-Study Schedule

NextStep TEST PREP | nextsteptestprep.com   Study Calendar   Test Day _____

	Monday	Tuesday	Wednesday	Thursday	Friday	Saturday	Sunday
WEEK 1	Take Diagnostic Test (June 2007 from PDF)	Review Diagnostic Test Diagnose weak areas	Learn Basic Linear Games Register for the test	Do a LG practice section UNTIMED Review section	Day Off	Practice Test 1 UNTIMED	Review Practice Test
WEEK 2	Basics of Logical Reasoning: -Question Types -Section Approach	Do a LR practice section untimed Review section	Structure of Arguments Review "Main Point" Questions	Do a LR practice section untimed Review section	Day Off	Practice Test 2 UNTIMED	Review Practice Test
WEEK 3	Intro to Reading Comprehension -How to approach -Basic strategies	Do a RC practice section untimed Review section	Basics of Conditional Logic The Contrapositive	Introduction to Grouping Games Do practice LG section TIMED	Day Off	Practice Test 3 TIMED	Review Practice Test
WEEK 4	Assumptions and assumption questions The Negation Test	Do a LR practice section TIMED Review section	Tricks of answer prediction in LR and RC LG Question Types review	Do a RC practice section TIMED Review section	Day Off	Practice Test 4 TIMED	Review Practice Test
WEEK 5	Multi-Axis Linear Games Practice Numbers and Percents on the LSAT	Do a LG practice section timed Review section	Common Flaws in LR Arguments Flaw Question Review	Do a LR practice section timed Review Section	Day Off	Practice Test 5 TIMED	Review Practice Test

 Study Calendar   Test Day _____

	Monday	Tuesday	Wednesday	Thursday	Friday	Saturday	Sunday
WEEK 6	Strengthen / Weaken Question Review	Do a LR practice section Review section	RC: Local Question Review LR Paradox Question Review	Do LR and RC practice sections timed Review sections	Day Off	Practice Test 6 TIMED	Review Practice Test
WEEK 7	Necessary / Sufficient Practice	Do a LR practice section Review section	If and Only If Review Formal Logic Practice	Do LG practice section timed Review section	Day Off	Practice Test 7 TIMED	Review Practice Test
WEEK 8	RC Global Question Review LR Method of Argument Questions	Do LR and RC practice sections timed Review sections	Parallel Reasoning and Parallel Flaw Questions	Do a practice LR section timed Review Section	Day Off	Practice Test 8 TIMED	Review Practice Test
WEEK 9	LR Inference Questions	Do a practice LR section timed Review Section	LR Principle Questions	Do a practice LG section timed Review Section	Day Off	Practice Test 9 TIMED	Review Practice Test
WEEK 10	RC Comparative Reading Passages	Do a practice RC section timed Review Section	LG Matching Games	Do a practice LG section timed Review Section	Day Off	Practice Test 10 TIMED	Review Practice Test

NextStep

Study Calendar   Test Day _____

nextsteptestprep.com

	Monday	Tuesday	Wednesday	Thursday	Friday	Saturday	Sunday
WEEK 11	Hybrid and Rare Games The Writing Sample	Do a LG practice section Review section	Practice Test 11	Review Practice Test 11	Day Off	Practice Test 12 TIMED	Review Practice Test
WEEK 12	Practice Test 13	Review Practice Test 13	Practice Test 14	Review Practice Test 14	Day Off	Test Day!	

ACKNOWLEDGMENTS

This is truly the kind of book that takes a village. My Facebook friends (past clients) have been incredibly generous in answering my requests for quotes and in allowing me to use their application materials as examples in this book. Special thanks to Lauren Morina (who compiled the "How to Use LSAC" materials), Jon Rausch (whose enthusiasm for volunteering whenever I need him is something I have come to depend upon), Lana Robins (for her extensive comments on a draft of this book), Ben Piiru (who generously volunteered every part of his law school applications to be shared in this book), Jeff Smith (whose ability to speak forum-ese has been a great help to me through the years), and many others.

I also have a great group of proofreaders on my staff who are essential to me in supporting my clients, and who have been incredibly helpful in reviewing drafts of this book and providing me with feedback. They include Max Alderman, Alli Hugi, Jane Jeong, and Emily Wilkinson, Charlotte Butash (who did a last-minute final edit on a Friday before a holiday weekend!) and especially Zoe Friedland, who initially came to me more than five years ago as a law school applicant, and over the years has become essential to me not only as an editor, but also as a friend.

I am indebted to my very good friend, Marni Lennon, who is insanely busy and committed to her work, as assistant dean, public-interest and pro bono director, and HOPE Public Interest Resource Center lecturer in law at the University of Miami, and who still made time to provide me with extensive and thoughtful commentary and suggestions to improve the book. It truly helps to have someone who thinks like me tell me what I forgot to say.

Special thanks to Nathan Fox and Ben Olsen for always being ready to provide me with a quote and for including me on their podcasts and in their LSAT prep classes on a regular basis. Thanks to Ronald Den Otter for providing me with materials and insights in this version and for being a great example of what a good prelaw advisor can offer to college students.

Thanks to those who helped with a previous edition of this book, because their input can absolutely be seen in this version as well: Elisha Alcantara, Ruth Bloom, Ronald Den Otter, Zoe Friedland, Jocelyn

Glantz, Elvira Kras, Nataly Laufner, Stephen Pedersen, Rebecca Sivitz, Jeff Smith, and Erin Staab.

Nothing happens at Law School Expert without the support and encouragement of my husband, Brent Levine. He's a partner in a law firm, a certified specialist in his area of practice, and he bends over backward to make sure I get through my busy law school application season without distractions. There's something incredibly attractive about a man dressed for court doing the laundry.

I have two daughters. I don't know that either of them will follow our examples and go to law school. But I do know they are growing up understanding what it is to work hard, to take care of others, and to find their purpose in the world. I thank them for all they do to inspire me and to make me laugh. Mostly, I thank them for reminding me what it is we are working toward and fighting for.

ABOUT THE AUTHOR

Ann K. Levine, Esq. is a law school admission consultant and the founder of Law School Admission Expert, Inc. (www.lawschoolexpert.com), which she established in 2004. In her thirteen years as a law school admission consultant, Ann has worked individually with more than two thousand applicants, and her Law School Expert blog has been read by hundreds of thousands of law school applicants. The first release of *The Law School Admission Game: Play Like an Expert*, published in 2009, became an Amazon.com best-selling law school guidebook. The second edition was published in 2013. She is also the author of *The Law School Decision Game: A Playbook for Prospective Lawyers*, in which she surveyed and interviewed more than 250 lawyers to compile advice for people considering attending law school.

After graduating *magna cum laude* from the University of Miami School of Law in 1999, Ann served as director of student services at the University of Denver College of Law, as director of admissions for California Western School of Law, and as director of admissions for Loyola Law School in Los Angeles. She is licensed to practice law in California and Colorado but no longer practices law—helping others reach their dreams has been her full-time gig since 2004.

Ann lives in Santa Barbara, California, with her husband (an attorney) and their two middle-school-aged daughters. You can follow Ann on Twitter **@annlevine** and connect with Ann on Facebook at the **Law School Admission Expert** page (https://www.facebook.com/LawSchoolAdmissionExpert/) for regular updates on law school–related news. Ann personally answers questions related to law school admission on her blog at www.lawschoolexpert.com/blog.

9 780983 845386